# CARAVAGGIO

**Text by Maurizio Calvesi**

Boy bitten by a lizard
*(1595), Florence, Longhi Foundation.*

# CARAVAGGIO

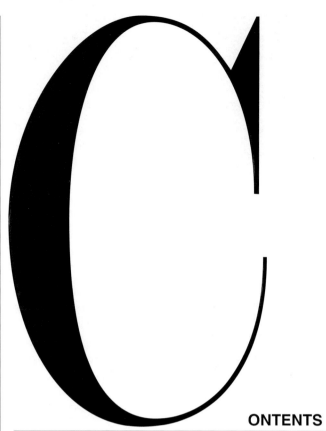

** C**ONTENTS

**Maurizio Calvesi**

**Cover:**
Bacchus
*(c. 1596-1597), detail.*
*Florence,*
*Uffizi Galleries.*

**Right:**
Head of Medusa
*(c. 1601-1602).*
*Florence,*
*Uffizi Galleries.*
**This wooden shield covered with painted canvas belonged to the armoury of Ferdinando de' Medici, where it was hung together with rich Oriental armour. It reached the Duke's collection via Francesco Maria del Monte, Tuscan ambassador in Rome and Caravaggio's protector.**

# PREMISE

The Deposition
*(1602-1604), detail.
Rome, Pinacoteca
Vaticana.*
**This painting was
conceived and
produced for Santa
Maria in Vallicella,
the church of the
Oratorians of San
Filippo Neri.
Probably,
Caravaggio's
introduction into the
Roman circle of the
Oratorians (or
Filippini) took place
under the auspices of
Cardinal Federico
Borromeo who was
practically a member
of the Oratory.**

# MICHELANGELO

Merisi, who was born in 1571 and died in 1610, was called "Caravaggio" after the small provincial town near Bergamo where he was brought up. His work is one of the highest expressions of art of all times and possibly the most passionately disconcerting. It is also the most heatedly debated.

The history of a painter is, by definition, rewritten every time it is newly interpreted, since every new interpretation modifies the image of what lies within the artist, of what is the source of his work. But never before and never since Caravaggio have interpretations of an artist been so discordant.

Even his contemporaries furiously "debated" his work and ferocious accusations were levelled against him. Nor can one say that he was unique in this. The world today is full of talented artists who have never really been understood and in the past this happened even with the best of artists. Michelangelo Buonarroti's *Universal Judgement* was the object of bitter accusations – both in religious and cultural circles – because of its supposedly "obscene" nudes. The most common recrimination in those days, in fact, was that of offending common decency and decorum; and for this Caravaggio was frequently reproached. However, whilst for Michelangelo Buonarroti these accusations have, with time, faded and his religious committment (whose profound philosophical value modern criticism has reappraised) has never again been questioned, for Michelangelo Merisi, only the way in which they are stressed has changed through the years.

People really believed that he was not only a violent rebel (as to some extent he undoubtedly was), but also that he contested religious doctrines (or was at best indifferent to their value), that he was "secular" (in the modern sense of the word) and that he was madly extravagant (some even claimed he was an epicurean). The trouble is that if it is true that his religion was art and that his cult was naked "reality", there is no longer a reason for condemning Caravaggio but rather for exalting him. Naked reality is what he would have liked to reproduce, stripping painting of all its added significance, anticipating the naturalism or realism of a painter like Courbet and classifying himself as a founder of a certain modernism seen as the triumph of individual freedom, as the cult of pure art, and also as "maledettismo".

# The Cursed Painter

Portrait of Caravaggio *by Ottavio Leoni (Rome 1578-1630). Florence, Marucellian Library.* **This drawing belongs to an album which collects together portraits of artists and important figures of the time in which Caravaggio lived in Rome. This is the most faithful likeness – apart from his self-portraits – we have of the artist.**

I T WAS IN 1884 THAT THE French poet, Paul Verlaine published his *Les Poètes maudits* (The Cursed Poets) which turned the established order of values upside-down and exalted writers such as Rimbaud (or himself) who saw poetry as something transgressive, an expression of an unruly existence which was at the same time self-destructive, precociously brilliant, unleashed, fatally extravagant, tempted by "evil", marked by poverty and by the suspicion of sexual perversion.

The image of Caravaggio as a "cursed painter", nurtured by the romantic atmosphere of this new ideology of art, became increasingly popular and took on all the suggestiveness which it maintains, at least as far as many critics and the majority of people are concerned, to this very day. But let us look more closely at how the literary sources (not always very reliable) and the documents of the time can help us *reconstruct* this image.

**POVERTY AND SOCIAL STATE**. "He managed to work his way out of his impoverished state with assiduous application", writes the Dutch Carel van Mander between 1600 and 1601 about Caravaggio. Giulio Mancini (1619) claims that "he lived off lettuce" when he first came to Rome, and likewise Bellori (1672) states: "When he came to Rome, he had no fixed abode and was totally at a loss as to what to do" and describes him as being "extremely needy and poorly clothed". Bellori goes on to say that his father was a "builder" and that Michelangelo himself, in the small town of Caravaggio, used to carry "revolting lime to the building-works" and occasionally had to "mix up the *paste* for painters to paint *a fresco*", which might well have been the starting point for his passion for painting. In point of fact, Fermo Merisi, Michelangelo's father, was a commissioned "house master" for the Marquises of Caravaggio, and was, however humbly, an architect, or so Mancini says; Baglione defines him as being of "fairly good family" (about 1625), as does Mancini when he claims "he was born of honourable citizens", whilst Joachim von Sandrart (who died in 1658) goes so far as to say he belonged to a "noble family".

We must conclude that the family was comfortably off, and belonged to the lesser nobility of the area. Documents, some of which have been unearthed only recently, seem to confirm this view. The Merisi family owned some land which the young orphan

Sick Bacchus
*(1593-1594), detail
of self-portrait. Rome,
Borghese Gallery.*
**In this painting the
artist seems to
portray himself after
a spell of sickness
spent in the Hospital
of the Consolation.
One can see signs of
his illness in the
patches of almost
bruised colour in his
face and in his
drained, anaemic
lips.**

Michelangelo sold on leaving for Rome when he turned twenty-one, toward the end of 1592. Furthermore, at his parent's wedding, the Marquis of Caravaggio was one of the witnesses. One of his brothers, Giovan Battista, went into the Church, following the example of their paternal uncle, Ludovico Merisi, who, after their parents's death, took custody over Michelangelo and went to Rome a few months before he did. When Michelangelo first set foot in the big city, therefore, he was not entirely without contacts, and – even if he did have some financial difficulties – he couldn't have been that desperate. As far as his initiation into the world of painting is concerned, this took place in 1585, when – as we can see in the contract – a thirteen year old Michelangelo was entrusted for a few years to a very well known master in Milan: the Bergamascan Simone Peterzano.

### HIS EXTRAVAGANT AND VIOLENT TEMPERAMENT.

All the sources seem to agree on this point. As early as 1600-01 van Mander writes: "if he works for a couple of weeks, he then goes off for a month or two with his sword by his side, followed by a servant-boy, from one ball-game to another, always ready for a skirmish or a duel ... his presence is in fact rarely tolerable".

The documents further demonstrate his restlessness. On the 19th of November, 1600, a certain Girolamo Stampa accuses Caravaggio of having assaulted him with a stick and threatened him with his sword; on the 28th of August, 1603, the painter Giovanni Baglione (his future biographer) takes Caravaggio and another friend of his, the architect Onorio Longhi, to court for having written scurrilous and defamatory verse against him; on the 24th of April, 1604, a waiter in a hostel charges him for throwing a plate of artichokes in his face; in October and November of the same year, on two separate occasions, Caravaggio was imprisoned for having used foul language against the police; on the 28th of May, 1605, he was arrested for illegal detention of arms; on the 29th of July of the same year, he was prosecuted for having attacked and actually wounded with his sword a public notary (Mariano Pasqualone) in a fight over women; in September, a certain Prudenzia Bruna lodged a complaint because Caravaggio had thrown stones at her window; on the 24th of October he was treated for sword-wounds which he claimed he had procured by falling on his own blade.

For Caravaggio, the 28th of May, 1606, represented the point-of-no-return. On this day, the painter murdered Ranuccio Tomassoni from Terni after a heated debate during a game of *pallacorda*, the equivalent of tennis at the time. The argument was over the umpire's decision on a foul, while they were playing facing the "ambassador of the Gran Duke (of Tuscany)", that is near *Palazzo Firenze*, where the street name (*via della Pallacorda*) goes back to the origins of the area as a playing-field. On Caravaggio's side, there was his companion Onorio Longhi, a certain Antonio da Bologna who was also fatally wounded in the struggle, and probably another painter friend, Mario Minniti. On Tomassoni's side there were three others about whom we know nothing. Amongst them, however (as a recent document reveals), there might have been the victim's brother who was the head of the *Rione Campo Marzio*.

Caravaggio, in this same brawl, procured a bad head injury and straight afterwards ran away from Rome, seeking refuge in the Latium estates of the Colonna family, his protectors.

We will never know whether it was the painter who struck his adversary first, or whether he was merely acting in self-defence. A detailed examination of the sources, nevertheless, reveals that Caravaggio was held entirely responsible for the incident; so much so that he was condemned to death by default. The death penalty

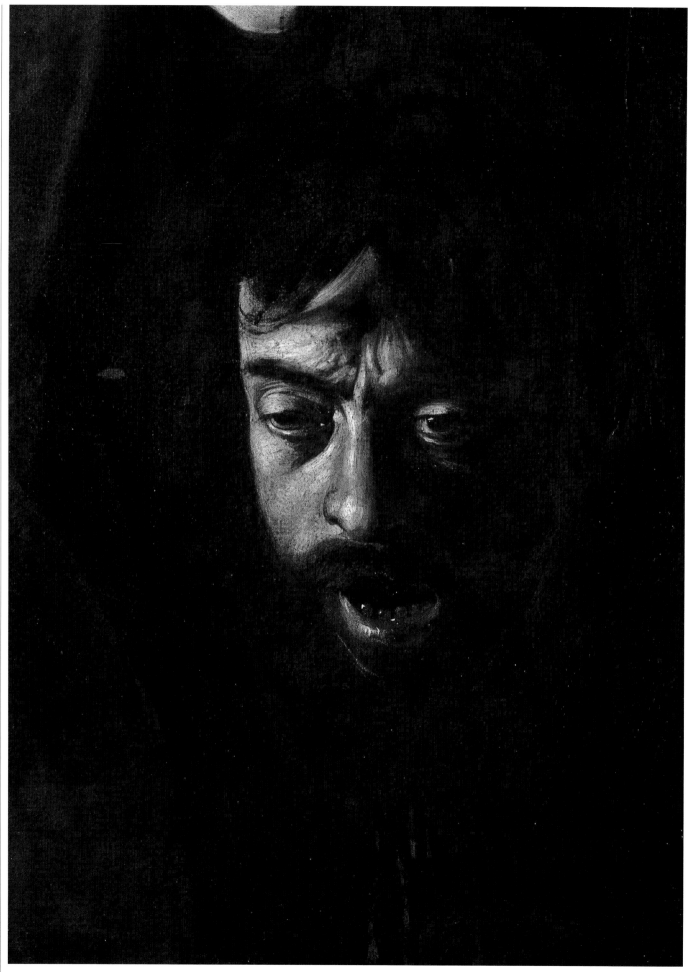

David with the Head of Goliath *(1610), whole painting and detail of self-portrait. Rome, Borghese Gallery.* **Caravaggio's last tormented years, spent as a fugitive to escape his capital sentence, are stamped on Goliath's face, on which one can see a sinister premonition of the end the artist foresaw for himself. A comparison with the self-portrait of the *Young Bacchus*, painted 16 years before, shows how profoundly events and constant tension had modified his very physiognomy.**

(or "capital ban") in those days was inflicted for much less than a murder, and implied that the defaulter could be arrested and put to death wherever he was. After a brief period of convalescence in the Colonna family's estates, Caravaggio ran away to Naples, and then to Malta where he was sent to prison, almost certainly because of the warrant of arrest from Rome. After escaping from prison (and we're now talking about 1608) he roamed from Syracuse to Messina, from Messina to Palermo; then in 1609 he reappeared in Naples, where he was assaulted by a group of men (most probably guards) and, on the point of death, he was again arrested.

However, someone in Rome took care of the Petition for mercy. Caravaggio, having been granted Papal pardon, went to the prison of Port'Ercole in July of 1610, probably under escort, in order to deal with all the complicated bureaucratic formalities for his discharge. He died soon after his release, while he was roving about on the beach, searching for the small boat which was supposed to take him back to Rome. The tragedy of the last four years of Caravaggio's life, during which he was no more than a hunted fugitive, was doubtless the reason for his "strange" behaviour which so many of his contemporary biographers put down to the eccentricity of his character. Francesco Susinno, a painter and writer from Messina, possibly picking up rumours which were still going around in the city, described him as follows: "He was an incredibly frenzied, disregardful kind of man, and certainly not very streetwise; he often went to bed with his clothes on, keeping his sword (which he never left anywhere) by his side because of the restlessness of his soul, which is more agitated than the Messina Strait with its dangerous currents which now rise and now fall. He dressed in a mediocre fashion, and (armed as he always was) he looked more like a cut throat than a painter. He was so weakminded and mad that there is little more one can say about him".

"That painter is out of his mind", noted in 1609 another local painter (a certain Niccolò di Giacomo) who had commissioned some paintings from Caravaggio.

But all this is easy to justify if we consider that when the artist was in Messina he must have lived in perpetual terror of being found, arrested and put to death, and if we allow for the deranging effect that the dramatic escape from Rome and subsequently from Malta and the endless roaming from one city to another, constantly alert and on guard, can't but have caused in him. It would be enough to compare the 1609 self-portrait (in which Caravaggio represents himself as Goliath beheaded by David, previsaging in a strange way the end he feared might befall him) to the youthful portrait (for instance *Little Bacchus*) of sixteen years before, to see the profound change that events had printed on his very physiognomy.

The Roman sources also stress Caravaggio's argumentativeness and his bizarre traits, but they don't go so far as to call him "mad". This further proves that it was only in the last few tragic years that he "was out of his mind". Mancini attributes to Caravaggio "some extravagance caused by that over-heated, magnanimous spirit of his", as early as the Milanese period. Similarly, von Sandrart, writes that "he was very whimsical and always ready for a fight". However, we must conclude that the much acclaimed madness and eccentricity of the unfortunate painter (which must have been difficult to decipher for people who knew nothing about his death-sentence) was implicitly connected to the fact that he was a fugitive, despite what the generalisations of generations of biographers claim. His existence had in fact been threatened by the tragic nightmare of death since he was a boy in Lombardy, when he lost both his grandparents and his father in the plague of 1577. There are certainly no doubts about his contentiousness, though one must bear in mind that at the time this behaviour was fairly

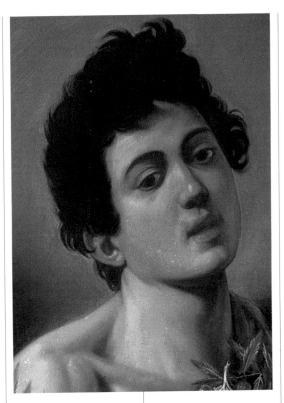

Youth with a Basket of Fruit
*(1593-1594), detail.
Rome, Borghese Gallery.*

**The suave, musical expression of the youth, with his lips parted as if to sing a song, evokes the theme of Love which we find again in the** *Young Saint John,* **in** *Rest on the Flight into Egypt* **and in** *Mary Magdalen.*
**In this youthful work one can see the traces of Merisi's formation in Lombardy: memories of Lotto, Savoldo, Peterzano and other Venetians, transcended in his subtle elegance which owes something to the sophisticated painting of the Flemish mannerists.**

common and that Caravaggio, therefore, was in no way exceptional. Take for example the famous English playwright, Christopher Marlowe (almost Merisi's contemporary), who was even more violent and disruptive than Caravaggio and died from a dagger-wound after a brawl. Or else, the poet Marino who practically lived in and out of prison and once became the target of Murtola's pistolshots. A blade once flashed even in Tasso's melancholic existence, against a servant who he was sure was spying on him. Cavalier d'Arpino, the prince of Roman painting was, like Caravaggio, condemned to death and subsequently pardoned. Saint Ignatius of Loyola himself had been a quarrelsome arms' bearer. And these are just a few of the many possible examples.

Leaving aside biographers in the past, the modern myth of Caravaggio as a "cursed painter" has always been sustained by a mistaken interpretation of his work. People have misinterpreted his "realism" which portrayed humanity as poor, anguished, repudiated, and therefore automatically, unconsciously to be considered as socially treacherous. They also misread the incredible contrasts of light and shade which are capable of evoking, even psychologically speaking, a feeling of shadows lurking. Finally the androgyny of the young artist's rather effeminate youths has always been a subject of open-ended interpretation.

**HIS PRECOCITY.** One of the attributes of Verlaine's vision of the "cursed" poet is that of precocity, as the tremendous example of Rimbaud illustrates. According to this logic, Caravaggio also had to be precocious, and this supposition has had a negative influence on the dating of the pictures.

Just recently new documents have allowed us to establish the fact that Merisi was born (in Milan, not in Caravaggio where he then lived) in 1571, almost certainly on the 29th of September, Archangel Michael his namesake's day.

Previously, it had always been thought that his date of birth was two years later, in 1573. Caravaggio, therefore, was supposed to be only eleven when he started his four-year apprenticeship under Simone Peterzano and only fifteen when he finished it before leaving for Rome. On the pavement of the Contarelli Chapel in San Luigi de' Francesi there is the date 1590, which was also attributed to the first of Caravaggio's largescale paintings in the same church. It had always been thought, then, that Caravaggio had received one of the most prestigious appointments in the artistic world of the time, undertaking what was to become a masterpiece at the tender age of seventeen. Only when more than one document was uncovered did critics surrender – after much resistance – to plain evidence: the paintings in San Luigi de' Francesi date back to 1599 or 1602, when Caravaggio was over thirty.

Biographers' testimonies (obviously for stylistic reasons) place a whole series of paintings before San Luigi de' Francesi, such as, for example, the *Little Bacchus* and the *Youth with a Basket of Fruit,* both in the Borghese Gallery in Rome.

These works had to be assigned, therefore, to the period between 1588 and 1590. And since everyone believed he was born in 1573, Caravaggio was thought to have painted some of his most refined works at the age of fifteen. In point of fact, he left his home-town at the end of 1592, and therefore painted those oils at the age of twenty-two.

To conclude, then, even in this respect Caravaggio was more normal than what one has always expected of him. "Genius" is not only a gift of Nature, it is also the product of application, research and intellectual maturity, just as the artist's "strangeness" was nothing to do with his nature, but was rather conditioned by the tragic events of his final years.

**HIS ATHEISM.** This is another connotation of the typology of the "cursed poet" which is very easy to identify in the nineteenth century, but not so easy to justify in the seventeenth century, and even less so in an artist like Caravaggio who produced so many altar-paintings. And yet critics have often claimed that he transgressed and scorned religious doctrines, basing their opinion on an emotional interpretation of his work and on the evidence of Susinno from Messina who said: "One day, as he walked into the church of the Madonna of Pilero with certain gentlemen, a man most kindly went up to the group to offer them holy water. When Caravaggio asked the man what it was for, the answer was 'to eliminate venial sins'. 'Well', said Caravaggio, 'then I don't need it, because my sins are all mortal'. The very fact that he goes around questioning our sacrosanct religion, when he is in no position to do so, gives him the reputation of an atheist, when even the Gentiles have always shown great respect for its mysteries". As Tacitus says "*Sanctius ac reverentius de actis deorum credere quam scirĕ*", and likewise Tertullianus – another wise father – "*Ignorare tutissimum est*" (that is, "As far as religion concerned, it is holier and more respectful to believe than to know"; "To be ignorant is the safest solution").

If Susinno's tardy tale isn't all made up or distorted, Caravaggio's zeal seems to have been simply in wanting to take part in theological discussions. The bitter comment on "venial sins", when his are "mortal", speaks for itself if we consider his deeply hidden secret: his death sentence. Moreover, documents demonstrate two precise facts: firstly that the painter took holy communion (as one can see in the *States of Mind* of San Nicola dei Prefetti, conserved in the Vatican Archives under the date of the 6th of June, 1605); and secondly, that in 1608, in Malta – *zelo religionis accensus* –, he became a *fratres milites* of the Order, undertaking to live under the rule of St. Augustine. A painting in Malta, the *Beheading of Saint John*, is signed "f(rà) Michel Angelo". The real reason why many modern critics have always sincerely believed that Caravaggio was an atheist, is different. The real reason is the fact that some of his paintings were not accepted as altarpieces for *decorum's* sake (or so the sources have always claimed). This will be discussed later. However, what we can say right away is that the accusations sprang from the supposed vulgarity of his figures. They were humble, lowly, sometimes earthy, with dirty feet. In fact, the debate wasn't so much between believers and non-believers, but rather between those who preached a "poor" Church (as in Caravaggio's case), and those who were terrified of these ideals which (if we wanted to use improperly a term taken from our political lexicon) we might define as being "left-wing". Critics have gone so far as to claim that Caravaggio, in reproducing sacred stories, went beyond the limits set by the Old and New Testament sources thus distancing himself from the official iconography. The mistake in this case is very easy to document since this distancing aimed if anything at an even more faithful reproduction of the dictates of the Bible or of the iconography of primitive Christian art, which fits perfectly with Caravaggio's aims and intentions when he exalted the poor and lowly. The Church, in the beginning, was a church for the poor, and some priests hoped for a return to its purity and to its ideals. Others did not.

**SUPPOSED SEXUAL PERVERSION.** This is another point over which interpreters's fantasies have been left free to roam, reproducing – yet again – the nineteenth century cliché of the "cursed poet". Critics tried to find some proof in the documents and literary sources of the time, going back to a further account of Susinno: "On holidays he would always hang around a grammar school teacher known as don Carlo Pepe who took his stu-

*Love Victorious (1602-1603). Berlin, Staatliche Museen Preussischer Kulturbesitz, Gemäldegalerie.*

**Those who believed that Caravaggio was a homosexual interpret the figure of Love in an erotic vein: the painter's "favourite" must have posed for him with complacent licentiousness. As a matter of fact, the splayed legs hark back to a symbolic code also used by Michelangelo to signify resurrection, victory and triumph.**

The Beheading of the Baptist
*(1608), detail.*
*La Valletta (Malta),*
*Oratoy of the Cathedral.*
**In 1608, in Malta, the painter became a member of the *fratres milites* of the Order of Saint John, submitting himself to the rule of Saint Augustine. It is for this reason that he signed this work "f(rà) Michel Angelo", dipping into the pool of blood flowing from the Baptist's wound. The last part of the signature is illegible due to the painting's having darkened.**

dents to the arsenal where once galley-ships were built but where now there are only the Portofranco deposits. Michael would wander around staring at the boys who were playing, in order to give shape to his fantasies. When the teacher got suspicious, he asked Michael why he always spent his time there. The proud painter was so outraged by this question that, in a furious temper – in order not to lose his reputation as a madman –, he gave the teacher a good thrashing over the head". If this story is not just another invention, one has to admit that a certain bias is necessary in supposing that phrase ("to give shape to his fantasies") alludes to the whims of a homosexual rather than, to the inspiration of an artist. Further proof is said to be provided by a document dated 28th of August, 1603, in which it is stated that the painter Filippo Trasegno had received a copy of the famous rhymes in which Onorio Longhi and Caravaggio teased Baglione: "Honorio and Micalangelo went to see a *bardassa* of theirs called Giovanni Battista". The word "bardassa" (or "bardascia") is a perorative which means "naughty boy" but it was often synonymous with "male prostitute". Again, however, the evidence is very shaky, and even if the word did refer to Caravaggio's homosexuality, one would still have to prove that the youth was his bedcompanion and not just a servant-boy. Onorio Longhi had a wife and five children, and as for Caravaggio, we know of at least two relationships with women, one with a Menicuccia, and one with a certain Lena. But the supporters of this hypothesis – so brilliantly worldly – also endorse a biography of Cardinal Del Monte, Caravaggio's principal protector, in which the churchman is described as being of loose morals and of poor culture. Fair enough, except for the fact that this particular biography was written by a political adversary, who wanted to justify the Spanish opposition to Del Monte's candidature for Pope (whereas this opposition was in fact caused by the pro-French militancy of the Cardinal, whose vast culture, furthermore, is well reknowned).

Lacking any more concrete evidence, critics have often brought the description of a party at Cardinal Damasceni Peretti's house into the picture: Del Monte and other Cardinals were present, and "since no women took part in the proceedings", the dancers were young boys dressed up as women. But this was perfectly normal: even in the theatre, the women's parts, to avoid the presence of those harbingers of temptation, were played by dressed-up men. In fact, Caravaggio's supposed homosexuality – vital as a final touch to the portrait of the "cursed poet" – is probably nothing more than a mistake. A mistake which arose from a dubious exegesis of some of the paintings from the early Roman period which show slightly effeminate figures, often considered provocative. For years, in fact, critics refused (and many still refuse) to interpret Caravaggio's work applying the "iconological" codes of the age. These allow one to appreciate his wonderfully revealing symbolism, which – despite his realistic approach – is an intrinsic part of his painting. If one doesn't understand the symbolic context, every single choice of subject for his paintings can be interpreted simply as the fruit of a spontaneous impulse; this leaves room for subjective and modernising reading of Caravaggio's work. The paintings in question are *Youth with a Basket of Fruit, The Lute Player, Concert, Bacchus, Rest on the Flight into Egypt.* Let's examine them, bearing in mind that the analysis of the altarpieces which follows will highlight an undoubtedly passionate religious commitment. These paintings were destined for private collections, which implies a difference both in their format and their tonality: sweeter and suaver than the "shady" and dramatic church canvases. We don't agree that these differences imply a radical movement away from all that is sacred and towards a winking wantonness (as some critics still believe) or towards a choice of subjects purely for their "genre", with no real significance (as other critics believe).

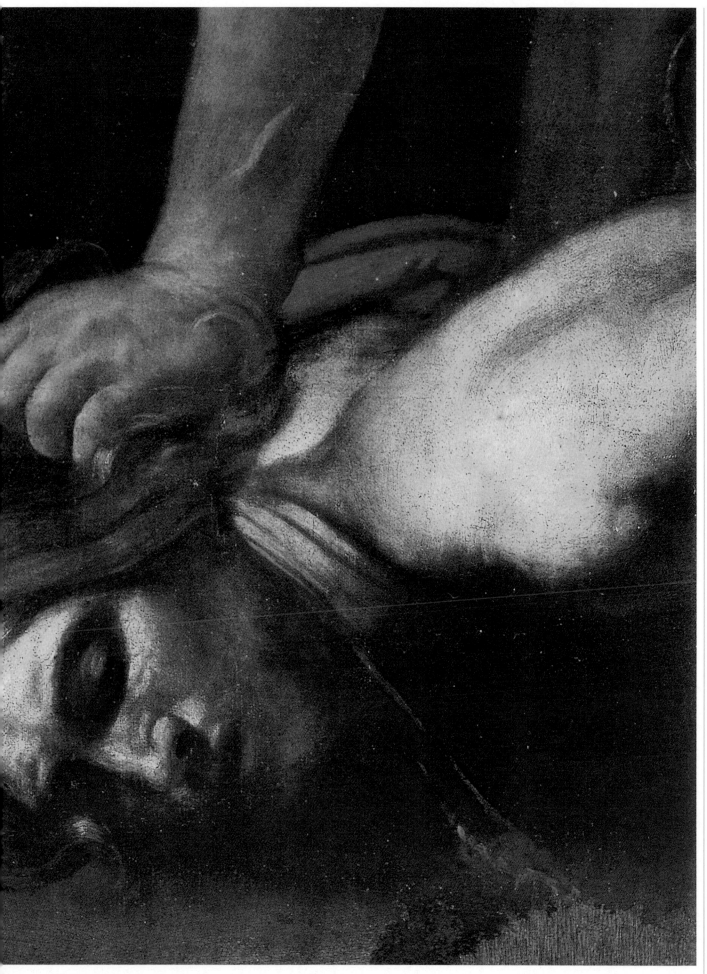

# Private commissions

**The smiling
expression of the
Saint seems to
communicate a sense
of "Christian
happiness" in the
spirit of the
Oratorians, followers
of San Filippo Neri.**

NE COULD START FROM
the *Young Saint John* which is probably the latest (about 1600) of the paintings mentioned, but exemplifies divergencies amongst critics.

Moir, who wrote a recent monograph of Caravaggio (1982), discredits the identity of the figure given by the old inventories. He claims that there are no attributes of Saint John which can be considered valid. "The old horned ram rubbing his nose against him is very different from the usual young lamb who trails behind him. The ram could symbolise lasciviousness, and the curious position of the boy straining forwards, with his legs splayed like Leda awaiting her swan, the expression on his face with its mocking grin, delicately veiled in shadow, the light so lovingly caressing his body – not to mention the artist's brushstroke – everything testifies against decency. Despite the fact that he is commonly accepted as Saint John, he is nothing but a pagan scoundrel untouched by religious sentiment".

This "reading" of the painting might be regarded as being – if not entirely acceptable – at least coherent with an interpretative logic if it were not for the fact that Caravaggio painted a further unconfoundable image of Saint John the Baptist, recognised by Moir as such: the one in the Borghese Gallery, where the ram features once again. There is no doubt however that the painting in the Capitoline Museum also represents the same saint, Jesus's cousin and childhood playmate, because he is depicted as sitting on a camelskin and a red cape, which are his traditional attributes.

To consider this image, so beautifully bathed in light like Michelangelo's nudes in the Sistine Chapel, indecent and unruly is a purely subjective judgement. By the same token, Michelangelo's nudes should appear obscene and slovenly, as in fact they were considered by censorious eyes at the time.

The legs are splayed, in an attitude inspired by Buonarroti's models, clearly decipherable according to the symbolic code of the time which Caravaggio has every reason to share. The raised leg indicates both the resurrection (in Christ's gesture as he steps out of his tomb with one foot), and victory, triumph (one can see the same gesture in Caravaggio's *Love Victorious*).

These two meanings are in harmony, because the resurrection triumphed over death, which in this painting is symbolised by the dried tree trunk on which the raised leg rests. In the upper right

Saint John the Baptist
*(1610). Rome, Borghese
Gallery.*

**On the opposite
page,**
Young Saint John
*(c. 1600). Rome,
Capitoline Museum.*
**According to some
critics, Caravaggio's
paintings
commissioned for
private collections are
mostly "genre
subjects" with no real
significance, or filled
with a desecrating
licentiousness. Thus,
the *Young Saint John* is
considered a pagan
ruffian untouched by
religious sentiment. A
comparison between
*Saint John the Baptist*
and the *Young Saint
John* shows the
correspondences
between the two
works which strictly
adhere to the sacred
theme: the light shed
on the ram and the
youth is the light of
Grace and Salvation
which conquers the
shadows of sin.**

hand corner, to reinforce the allegory, green vine-leaves (a common Christological symbol of eternal life) wink at one out of the darkness.

In the *Saint John the Baptist* in the Borghese Gallery one can also see vine-leaves in the background, and the raised foot resting on a dried tree trunk. These cannot therefore be chance details; they must have been chosen for their significance.

The canvas, as a matter of fact, alludes to Divine Love in virtue of which humanity was saved from Christ's holocaust. The lamb which traditionally accompanies Saint John is the personification of Jesus. Even the ram – as any most elementary book on Christian iconography would tell you – stands for Christ; his horns were a sort of "hieroglyph" for the Cross. In the catacombs, the sacrifice of Isaac was always represented with a ram by Isaac's side, signifying, as Saint Augustine taught, that his sacrifice prefigured Christ's. Often the ram was put side-by-side with Jesus's monogram. By replacing the more common image of the lamb with that of a ram, Caravaggio wanted to call attention to the symbolism of the early Christians, as Federico Borromeo – a believer in the Church's return to the purity of its origins – had always highly recommended. He certainly didn't want to introduce a note of lasciviousness. The tame animal goes as if to rub his nose against the cheek of the saint, who is embracing him. This movement alludes to the bond of affection between the two divine cousins, but also – and above all – to the reciprocal love between Christ and redeemed Humanity. In the bottom left hand corner there is a spark of flame in the wood, framed by the red cloak: both the fire and the colour of the drapery evoke the ardour of that divine sentiment of love.

But it is the light which falls on the sacred animal and on the young boy's body making it seem radiant and polished, as if in a dazzling revelation, and which highlights out of the depths of shadow the triumphant *chiaroscuro* of the greens, whites and reds; it is the light which is the most important and most expressive symbol of all: the light of Grace and Salvation, which conquers the shadow of sin.

It is this basic symbolic imagery which was at the heart of Caravaggio's invention of light. Light became Caravaggio's stylistic manifesto which revolutionised the painting of the time, and managed to reconcile the two opposite extremes of the chromatic, luminous pictoricism of the Venetian school, and the Tuscan-Roman "drawing" of Raphael and Michelangelo. His light has a plastic quality which makes the figures rounder, burning away all traces of the drawing, and at the same time exalts their tangible three-dimensionality and gives the colour a crystal clear and yet fluid intensity. The saint's smiling expression is not at all "mocking"; it communicates, rather, a feeling of "Christian happiness" – to use the expressions of the orators of San Filippo Neri – of "happiness" and "exultance".

There is no doubt that Caravaggio's capacity to *feel* has a direct impact on the tension of the senses. But it is precisely in this radical synthesis of idealism and physical plenitude and in the absolutely "incarnated" quality of the symbols and of the light itself, which is both real and unreal (as we shall see, the light sources are never actually indicated), that the "grandeur" of the artist lies. The symbol loses its abstract quality and becomes incorporated in a clear picture of natural reality, read with great attention. The ram is Christ, but this does not mean that it is no longer a true-to-life ram. This is valid for each and every symbol used by Caravaggio: it is precisely in the flagrancy of reality that one can find the flagrancy of the symbol. His "realism" is not an end in itself as it has often been judged to be, by those who project onto a sixteenth-seventeenth century painter a way of con-

ceiving art and reality itself which is really only relevant to the nineteenth and twentieth century. The Renaissance artist, whose culture still had a strong influence on Caravaggio, saw reality on earth as being a mirror, however obscure, of a superior power which communicates through signs in Nature itself and through the "numinous" light which reveals all.

The *Supper in Emmaus* (in the National Gallery, London), painted more or less at the same time as the *Young Saint John*, demonstrates once and for all Caravaggio's *penchant* for the symbol. The disciples recognizes their resurrected Christ as he blesses the bread, initiating the sacrament of the Eucharist. The depth of the luminous space which wedges itself into the shade, is tested in a masterly fashion by the positioning of the objects on the table right up to the fruit-basket which topples over the edge. The apostle on the left, who – in his surprise – is about to push himself up with his hands on the chair-arms, is positioned even closer to the eye of the observer and acts as a "bumper" to the perspective. The compact use of the space – almost a parallelepiped of light – is interrupted by the Redemptor's hand held forwards, and boldly limited by the apostle's open-armed gesture, which seems to sustain the whole right-hand-side of the picture, stretching across the whole depth of the painting like the heavy disappearing-line of a trunk or of a beam.

This gesture, in fact, alludes precisely to the solid architecture of the cross according to a code which was well-rooted in tradition, and followed by Masaccio and Michelangelo. The apostle recognizes the Lord, and in that very moment his arms imitate the supreme model of the cross. The resurrected Christ turns out to be not so much the mature man one would expect of his age, but rather a young man with an androgynous face, half male-half female, similar to the paleo-Christian images of the Good Shep-

Supper in Emmaus
(c. 1600). London,
National Gallery.

**This painting unmistakably demonstrates the use of symbolism: the bread blessed by Christ alludes to his body and the wine to his blood. The disciple with his arms outstretched (as if to measure space), while he recognizes the Lord, mimes in his gesture the shape of the cross.**

herd. Youth is a sign of the eternal life which Christ offers to his followers; androgyny is a sign of the "union of opposites" on which perfect harmony is founded. As Scotus Eriugena wrote in the ninth century, "Jesus is himself a unity which contains the division of nature, that is the division between male and female. He rose from the dead not in a bodily sex, but only in Man; in him there is neither male nor female". Cardinal Federico Borromeo recommended that Christ's face should resemble Mary's.

The dining table is also full of allegorical references. Christ's act of blessing the bread means that it becomes the symbol of his body, whilst obviously the wine which one can see in the glass decanter becomes his blood. Following the canonic rules for representing the table-altar, next to the bread and wine there is a dead animal which represents Christ's sacrifice. It could have been a lamb or a fish, in this case it is a chicken (or hen) which stands for the evangelical figure of Jesus. Given the context, the fruit basket, thrust so obviously into the observer's view, in the typically dominant position awarded to particularly "significant" objects, must also be read in an allegorical key.

And so we see that the basket contains grapes and pomegranates, common emblems of Christ's martyrdom, and apples which allude both to the "fruits" of grace and to the original sin from which humanity has been redeemed.

Writings of the Fathers of the Church positively gush with annotations which explain, the symbolic and Christological value of fruit. One text in particular lends itself to this theological exegesis: the *Song of Songs*, a poem – in fact profane though it has always been considered sacred and allegorical – which sings of the love of the Groom (Christ) for his Bride (the Madonna, standing for the Church, or for Humanity itself). In fact, the prayers of the Virgin derive from the lines of the poem.

Supper in Emmaus *(c. 1600), detail. London, National Gallery.*
**Given the context, even the basket of fruit must be read in an allegorical vein: it contains grapes and pomegranates (common emblems of Christ's martyrdom) and apples, which allude both to the fruits of Grace brought by Christ and to original sin. The incredible naturalism of the fruit, its turgid and life-like plasticity rendered by the crystalline and mobile touch of light, does not deny, but rather gives weight to the hypothesis of a Symbolic universe.**

Rest on the
Flight into Egypt
*(c. 1599). Rome, Doria
Pamphilj Gallery.*

The amazing naturalism of Caravaggio's painted fruit, its full-bodied and palpitating plasticity which derives from the crystalline but mobile shedding of light, doesn't deny this interpretation. In fact it backs it even further: following the logic of the intense poetic communion with what is "numinous" in nature. In order to find support for the symbolic interpretation of the images of fruit and flowers so recurrent in Caravaggio's early works, the Author of this "dossier" went back to find some quotations from the *Song of Songs*.

Recently, however, a reference to a transcription of Merisi's has been firmly established. A group of musicologists have in fact managed to decipher the sheet of music which appears in the *Rest on the Flight into Egypt* (in the Doria Gallery in Rome), it has been found to be a celebratory motet for the Virgin composed by a Franco-Flemish musician called Nöel Baul Dewijn, which uses some lines from the *Song of Songs*:

> *"Quam pulchra es et quam decora,*
> *charissima, in deliciis!*
> *Stature tua assimilata est palmae,*
> *et ubera tua botris.*
> *Caput tuum est Carmelus,*
> *collum tuum sicut turris eburnea.*
> *Veni, dilecte mi, egrediamur in agrum;*
> *videamus si flores fructus parturiunt,*
> *Si florebunt mala punica;*
> *ibi dabo tibi ubera mea".*

**The sweet music played on the violin by the angel is evoked by the diffusion of light, graded into incredibly fine shades. The contrast between the harmonious youth of the divine figures (the angel and the Virgin with the sleeping Child) and the rugged "human" figure of Joseph is like that between light and shadow.**

The first 6 lines are dedicated by the Groom to the Bride and are therefore referred to the Madonna:

> *"Behold thou art fair, my love;*
> *O thou fairest among women!*
> *This thy stature is like to a palm tree*
> *and thy breasts to clusters of grapes.*
> *Thine head upon thee is like Carmel*
> *Thy neck is as a tower of ivory".*

The last 4 lines are spoken by the Bride to the Groom:

> *"Come, my beloved, let us go forth into the field,*
> *Let us see if the vine flourish*
> *whether the tender grape appear:*
> *There I will give thee my loves".*

In the painting the sweet music being played on the violin by the angel is evoked once again by the diffusion of light, so delicately graded from incredibly sunny to incredibly soothing.

On Joseph's face, sun scorched and tried by old age, the wrinkles have been realistically marked whilst the other figures – the angel with his instrument, the Virgin with the sleeping Baby – seem smoothed down, Apollonian, in contrast. This contrast, calling to mind the very opposition between light and shade, is an effect which Caravaggio repeats over and over again: the harmonious youthfulness of the divine figures, and the harsh, hollowed-out consumption of the human figures.

Even the two halves of the picture present a contrast, which is quite common in Renaissance art. The left-hand side, where Joseph is sitting, is closed-in, arrid and rock-strewn; the right-hand side is invaded with light and opens out onto a bucolic river scene, with Mary surrounded by lush vegetation, a sign of Life and of the abundance of divine Grace. The link is provided by a huge dessicated tree which brings Death to mind. But it is through death (a joyous event, according to San Filippo Neri) that one passes from the difficult terrestrial world to the paradisaical kingdom of Eternity. And this is what the flowers and fruit in the *Song of Songs* and the greenery which surrounds the Virgin allude to. It is highly likely that whoever commissioned this painting had something to do with the *Oratoriani* (or *Filippini*, followers of San Filippo Neri) who took great interest in music, and to whom Caravaggio as we will see was very close.

The Oratorian church, inaugurated in May 1599 (more or less at the same time as when the *Rest on the Flight into Egypt* is presumed to have been painted) has on its façade a line from the *Song of Songs*, which is very similar to the one transcribed by Caravaggio *"tota pulchra es, amica mea, et macula non est in te"* ("Thou art all fair, my love; there is no spot in thee"). The church, dedicated to the Madonna, was christened "Santa Maria in Vallicella" because the River Tiber a few months previously had flooded the area making it into a little river valley. The valley here painted by Caravaggio could well be a lyrical recollection of this fact.

The Virgin Mary, embracing her beloved "Groom" (Jesus), has fallen asleep as if exhausted at the end of a long day. This detail is delicately poetic, but it is also clearly referred to other lines of the *Song*. "I languish in love" says the Bride, asking her Groom to "place your left hand under my head and embrace me with your right". And again, "I sleep, but my heart is vigilant". "I charge you, O daughters of Jerusalem, that ye stir not up, nor awake my love, until she pleases" says the Groom. According to the Patristic tradition, it is the love for the Groom Jesus, and the intoxication of Celestial Mysteries which make the Bride (i.e. the Madonna, in which the Church itself was identified) languish into sleep.

"The hair on your head is like the purple of a King" claims the Groom; and in fact the Virgin's full head of hair tends towards red in Caravaggio's painting. The fathers of the Church interpret

Rest on the
Flight into Egypt
*(c. 1599), detail. Rome,
Doria Pamphilj Gallery.*

**A group of musicologists have deciphered the musical scores and recognized in them a motet composed by a Franco-Flemish musician picking up some lines of the *Song of Songs* in which the Groom and the Bride are identified with Jesus and Mary.**

Rest on the Flight
into Egypt
*(c. 1599), detail. Rome,
Doria Pamphilj Gallery.*
**The Virgin, hugging
her loving "Groom"
Jesus, has fallen
deeply asleep,
exhausted after a
long day. The
delicately poetic
annotation is inspired
by two lines of the
same *Song of Songs*: "I
sleep, but my heart is
vigilant".**

**On the opposite
page:
Immersed and
exhausted by Love
and Grace, the *Mary
Magdalen* is very close
to the *Rest*. The light
of Salvation shines on
the repentant sinner
and redeems her
highlighting in its
luminous cone her
submissive human
condition. On the
floor lie the
abandoned pearls
and necklaces.**

the king's purple as being the delivering blood, offered by the Redeemer. The whole painting thus evokes the theme of Christ's
Salvation, by virtue of his Grace, symbolised by the same light.
This is, as we shall see further on, a central theme in Caravaggio's
entire repertory.
Similar to the Bride in the *Song of Songs*, and immersed in the las-
situde of Love and Grace, is the *Mary Magdalen* (in the Doria
Gallery in Rome), which is very close to the *Rest*. The light of salvation, exemplified in the top part of the painting by a shaft of
light which modulates the refined monochromatic quality of the
background shines on the repented sinner, redeeming her. The
sharply-defined luminous cone patrols the figure from all sides
analysing her humble, human condition and at her feet lies the
abandoned jewellery, next to the jar of unguent with which she
went to the rescue of the loved Lord. The lines of the woman's
body all play together to contribute to the feeling of sweet aban-
donment to sleep, while her face is still stained by a teardrop of
repentance. "Amore langueo" ("I languish with love") is written
in the ray of light which shines on the Magdalen in a painting of
a Sicilian follower of Caravaggio's, Monocolo di Racalmuto.
If we now take a step backwards and analyse the oils painted by
Caravaggio when he first came to Rome (that is around 1593),
we come across *The Youth* in the Borghese Gallery, who holds in
his arms a basket of fruit very similar to the one in *Supper in Emmaus*, though it contains a greater variety of fruit (for instance
there are figs, grapes, pomegranates and apples). It is precisely
this variety and analytic descriptiveness which show how much
time lapsed between the two paintings, and demonstrate how

Mary Magdalen
*(c. 1599). Rome, Doria
Pamphilj Gallery.*

Youth with a Basket
of Fruit
*(1593-1594). Rome,
Borghese Gallery.*
**An analytic
descriptiveness
and a lesser force
in the contrasts
between light and
shade are what
characterise
Caravaggio's early
painting.
The work is anyway
extraordinary
because of the
sensitivity of the**

much less synthetic the early Caravaggio was.

Similarly, the light is not as volumetrically defined; it brushes the figure with much less innovative *chiaroscuro* and contrast. Nonetheless, the work is extraordinary because of the naturalistic sensitivity with which the silent life of the magic fruit is evoked, because of the masterly use of *penombra* which grades the positioning of the leaves in space, and because of the exquisite intensity of the colour references, from the matt black of the youth's hair and eyes to the glossier black of the grapes, from the whites touched by grey to the toned-down greens, and the various ranges of red.

One can see in the painting traces of Caravaggio's cultural formation in Lombardy: memories of Lotto and his illuminism (though he transcended him in his subtle elegance), of Savoldo or Peterzano, not to mention a good knowledge of the Venetians, from Giorgione to Titian, and also of the Tuscan preciosity of Bronzi-

**naturalistic details
with which the silent
life of the magic fruit
is evoked.**

no, but, above all, of the sophisticated Flemish mannerists such as Van Aachen. The influence of the Flemings on the young Caravaggio has certainly always been underestimated: the same Flemings which the Cardinals Francesco Maria Del Monte and Federico Borromeo so loved. The suave and musical expression of the boy, with his lips parted to whisper a word, or sing or listen to a song, brings immediately to mind the theme of Love which we found in the *Mary Magdalen*, in the *Rest* and in the *Young Saint John*: spiritual and sacred love, despite the fact that it seems so steeped in sensuality. It is a sensuality which tends towards idealism, a typical weakness at the time. There is no need even to consider the undoubtedly erotic raptures (which are sincerely religious and aim at transcendency) of Saint Teresa of Havilant, who died ten years before; it is sufficient to go back to the *Song of Songs* which is in this respect symptomatic. In this text, the expression of sweetened yet intense eros used as a parameter for the love for Jesus which transforms any tension in the senses into pure metaphysical contemplation.

Whoever believes in Caravaggio's homosexuality sees a sign of it in these effeminate figures. We've already talked, however, about the "divine" meaning of androgyny, which was anyway clearly visible before Caravaggio's time in some of Leonardo's figures (amongst others) which are without a doubt sacred. The Groom in the *Song of Songs* was considered to be androgynous; his attributes were even believed to be completely interchangeable with the Bride's, just as the attributes of Christ and of the Church are interchangeable. Sweetness is a prerogative of the Groom, and the *Song* in fact evokes milk, honey, spices and oils. The languid boy's pose recalls that of the Groom. The Bride says:

> *"My beloved is white and ruddy*
> *the chiefest among ten thousand.*
> *His locks are bushy and black as a raven...*
> *As the apple tree among the trees of the wood,*
> *So is my beloved among the sons.*
> *Stay me with flagons,*
> *Comfort me with apples,*
> *for I am sick of Love".*

And the Groom says:

> *"The fig tree putteth forth her green figs,*
> *and the vines with the tender grape*
> *give a good smell.*
> *Arise, my love, my fair one,*
> *and come away.*
> *I will go up to the palm tree,*
> *I will take hold of the boughs thereof:*
> *now also thy breasts shall be as clusters of the vine,*
> *and the smell of thy nose like apples".*

In the fruit-basket of the *Song of Songs* then, apart from pomegranates, grapes and a wide variety of apples, there are also figs, just as in Caravaggio's basket. The same themes are repeated, as, for example, in the closure of the seventh chapter:

> *"At our gates are all manner of pleasant fruits*
> *new and old, which I have laid up for thee,*
> *O my beloved".*

It's hard to imagine the youth in the Borghese Gallery as anything other than a personification of the Groom; that is, an allegory of Christ as a boy, bearer of the loving fruits of Grace. These works were mostly destined for the clergy or Cardinals, and when Caravaggio, brother and nephew of two church-men, first arrived in Rome, he lodged first with one Monsignor (Pandolfo Pucci) and then with another (Fantin Petrignani), and finally he was welcomed into a Cardinal's home, that of Del Monte. Another Cardinal, the Oratorian Ottavio Parravicino, defined some paintings of

Sick Bacchus (1593-1594). Rome, Borghese Gallery.

**In this painting, Caravaggio seems to have portrayed himself after a period of illness. The sophisticated Christological significance of the subject, however, makes one think of a sort of *ex voto* or wish for his own "resurrection".**

Bacchus
*(c. 1596-1597).*
*Florence, Uffizi*
*Galleries.*

**Likewise Bacchus might well be a sophisticated, intellectual allusion to the Groom in the *Song of Songs*. The myth of Bacchus/Dionysus, who died and was born again, was considered by the Neo-Platonists a mysterious prefiguration of the Redeemer. The delicate suspension of silence created by the light surrounds the grapes, apples, figs and pomegranates, which again seem to have been taken out of the fruit-basket in the *Song*.**

Caravaggio's in a letter dated 2nd of August, 1603, as «half devoted, half profane». This phrase seems to be highly pertinent to his juvenile works, where the underlying devotion is extraordinarily light-weight, thanks to a pleasing poetic metamorphosis. Amongst Caravaggio's earliest works in Rome, the most remarkable is the *Sick Bacchus* (in the Borghese Gallery, Rome) which is clearly a self-portrait. Caravaggio had spent a period of illness in the Hospital of the Consolation: one feels one can see the signs of this illness both in the ashy colour of his face and in his drained anaemic lips. Against the dark background, the figure of Bacchus is cast in light, though the muscles in the half-naked body are still hinted at by the more traditional *chiaroscuro*. On the other hand, incredible attention has been paid to the intense and opaque quality of colour: the touch of bright yellow in the two peaches lying near the black grapes in the foreground; the green of the ivy crown against the raven black hair; the deep, dark-brown eyes; the white and purplish colour of the drapes which barely cover him. Bacchus looks benumbed: his face crossed by a painful sneer, one hand holding the bunch of grapes up to his mouth, the other reaching forwards as if to pick one of the golden or greenish berries. The care endowed on the colouring of the fruit and on the differing sizes of the grapes (one of which has shrivelled up) or on the varying luminousity of the ivy-leaves (one of which has wilted) confirm our impression of Caravaggio's desire to reproduce nature in its every detail. Bacchus's face, so psychologically intense and whose every-wrinkle bears a connotation, further demonstrates this. The subject is unusual: the crown of ivy and the grapes make us think of Bacchus's attributes; even more so because Caravaggio painted another picture using the same subject which we will now examine. But whilst ever-green ivy is a common symbol of eternal life, we all know the Christological significance of grapes in Merisi's early work. The youth's raised left leg seems to suggest again the interpretation (remember *Young Saint John*) of elevation and resurrection. Likewise, the reflection of the black grapes in the golden bunch seems to hint at the transition from death to life. Caravaggio seems to have portrayed himself after his spell in hospital almost as if the painting were an *ex voto* or a wish, alluding to his own "resurrection" in the subtly sophisticated hermetically sealed cult of the devoted "imitation" of the Lord. In fact, even the *Bacchus* in the Uffizi Galleries (a later work by a few years) is certainly not lacking in cultured and intellectual allusions to Christ himself, if not to the Groom in the *Song*. The myth of Bacchus, the Greek Dionysus (who died and was born again) lent itself to deeper interpretation: he was a prefiguration or a mysterious announcement of the coming of the Redemptor. According to Marsilio Ficino, a champion of Renaissance Neo-Platonism, Bacchus incarnates the first level of divine fervour, the priest who deals with the mysteries of sacrifice. Pico della Mirandola, likewise, wrote: "in revealing to us the invisible signs of God and his mysteries, that is the invisible signs of Nature, Bacchus intoxicates us with the cornucopia of the House of the Lord, in which Holy Theology, taking us over, will charge us with a double fervour". Ficino and Pico, to conclude, playing on the homonym of "Dionysus" give the name "Christian Dionysus" to San Dionigi Aeropagita, who dipped the Vision of the Sacred Mysteries, or the "mysteria dionysiaca", "into the drunkenness of this dionysiac wine".

It is interesting to note that San Dionigi Aeropagita was confused with San Dionigi, Bishop of Paris, Patron Saint of France, and that the church of San Luigi de' Francesi, in which Caravaggio was to produce his first large-scale public commission procured for him by Cardinal Del Monte, was dedicated to Aeropagita himself. *Bacchus* was probably painted for Del Monte who was an Italian ambassador for the French nation and always boasted that he

Bacchus
*(c. 1596-1597), detail.
Florence, Uffizi
Galleries.*
**The theme of
"spiritual
drunkenness",
elaborated by the
Fathers of the Church
in their comments
regarding the *Song*, is
again proposed by
Bacchus who offers a
goblet full of wine.**

descended from the king of France. The Christian "Dionysus" must have been a cherished subject for him.

Neo-Platonism derived from Ficino was very much in fashion in France at the time. It is easy to trace back some of Caravaggio's codes to this philosophy: his use of light, the spiritual theme of Love, the refined hermetic culture cultivated by Del Monte which Christianised pagan symbols, and alchemy.

But this Neo-Platonic hermetism with all its ambiguous references to the "mysteria dionysiaca", was nothing more than a reworking of the theme of "spiritual intoxication" elaborated by the Church Fathers in their comments on the *Song of Songs*. Phrases exchanged between the Bride and the Groom such as:

Bacchus
*(c. 1596-1597), detail.*
*Florence,*
*Uffizi Galleries.*

**The androgyny of Bacchus, again considered to be proof of Caravaggio's paederastic tendencies, more probably alludes to the "union of opposites" by which perfect harmony can be achieved.**

*"Thy navel is like a round goblet,*
*which wanteth not liquor".*
*"I have drunk my wine with my milk:*
*eat, o friends; drink yea,*
*drink abundantly".*

were unanimously considered to recall the words of the Gospel: "then, taking the cup, he gave it to them saying: take, drink, this is my blood of alliance". Saint Ambrogio annotated: "The Mysterious cup is as if enriched by the author of our Faith; it is more than perfect, and always brimming over with a spiritual and heavenly liquor, since the Church has wine in its cup, which lightens man's heart".

Finally, Cesare Ripa, author of the manual *Iconologia* which contains a eulogy of Cardinal Del Monte and which defines Bacchus as "a symbol of divine intellect", writes under the entry "Grace" (bringing to mind the Groom's phrase): "the cup denotes Grace, according to the Prophet, *Calix meus inebrians quam praeclarus est.* The words *Bibite, et inebriamini* (drink yea, drink abundantly) can be used because whoever is in God's grace is always drunk with the sweetness of His love; this intoxication is so strong and so vigorous that it assuages the thirst for worldly objects".

The effeminate attributes of the *Bacchus* have obviously been considered a proof of Caravaggio's paederastic propensities. His divine androgyny, however, should be considered on a level with the *Youth* in the Borghese Gallery. Similarly, in the *Song of Songs* we can find surprisingly corresponding descriptions, such as:

*"His locks are bushy and black as a raven...*
*his arms are as the most fine gold,*
*his belly is as bright ivory".*

With one finger of his left hand, knotted in a black bow, the young Bacchus points at his umbilicus ("knot", or centre, "onfalus", Neo-Platonically the "nodus mundi"), and with his right hand he holds forward the wine goblet, as if to stress the relationship suggested in the *Song* ("Thy navel is like a round goblet, which wanteth not liquor") visualising his invitation to drink and get drunk. The numinous wine is presented in the terse glass goblet magically touched by light, again near the fruit basket full of grapes (arso on his head-garland), apples, figs and pomegranates: the fruit of the *Song of Songs*.

The incredibly delicate silent suspension created by the light seals the sacred atmosphere of the "mysteria dionysiaca".

In other paintings of the same period (such as *The Lute Player* in Leningrad, and *The Concert* in New York) the effusion of light is like the evocation of music: it is an instrument of spiritual elevation and a metaphor for "tuning" or "harmony" in the Platonic tradition of Love (indicated in the music-sheets). The presence of flowers and fruit, moreover, symbols according to the Church Fathers with celestial significance (the iris, the daisy, the rose, the pear, the grape) reinforce this idea.

The *Boy Bitten by a Lizard*, on the other hand, contains a clear moral warning: behind the delights of pleasure (the cherries), lurks the trap of the Lizard, symbol of suffering, there is no rose without a thorn, or again, pleasures in life are by necessity brief since death is always ready to attack.

Amongst Caravaggio's works previous to his first public commission for San Luigi de' Francesi, one in particular is of interest: a ceiling decoration in Cardinal Del Monte's laboratory of alchemy. This work (around 1597) shows Caravaggio's utter familiarity with the allegorical genre and with Neo-Platonic hermeticism. Pluto, Neptune and Jove are so effigied as to represent the various phases of the transmutation of substance (corresponding to the elements of earth, air and water) by which the "philosophical stone" (a hieroglyph of the Universe and, in imitation of *Genesis*, of light itself) can be gendered.

One more work belongs to the category of private commissions, and that is *The Basket* (in the Pinacoteca Ambrosiana, Milan). It is considered to have been painted during the San Luigi de' Francesi years because of the marvellous and masterly achievement of the representation of the fruit, startling in its plasticity and luminosity. Here is another isolated example of that image which came to mind observing the *Youth* of the Borghese Gallery, the *Bacchus* and the *Supper in Emmaus*. Hand in hand with the sense of vigorous growth inherent in the description "from all sides", goes the elegance of the arrangement, the measured quality which contains the vigour, and which, again, has something of the Renaissance balance and of the plastic illuminism of someone like Antonello da Messina. The light which seems to come from more than one source is like a life-giving breath of air, which moves twigs and leaves, and turns colour into perfume. The painting belonged to Cardinal Federico Borromeo from 1607. In fact, he almost certainly commissioned it. Borromeo, who lived in Rome from 1586 to 1595, was elected in that year Archbishop of Milan (following his cousin San Carlo), but he went back to live in Rome from April 1597 to May 1601. His favourite genre above all others, was the still life, which was just emerging at the time, and for Borromeo the Flemish Jan Brueghel painted some still lives of flowers. Maybe it was Borromeo himself, therefore, who asked Caravaggio to paint this basket of fruit. In the church of San Clemente, run by the Ambrosian Congregation in Milan, in the twelfth century apse mosaic there are two symbolic baskets full of pomegranates and other fruit in amongst the twines of vine-leaves which surround the crucifix. Borromeo himself in his book *De Pictura Sacra* written for painters praises "that famous and wonderful work in the church of San Clemente". The chapter of the Ambrosians, in fact, was presided over by an *alter ego* of his: the oblate of Sant'Ambrogio, Antonio Seneca.

Right next door to the home of the oblates of Sant'Ambrogio in Milan, Borromeo had the Ambrosian Palace built where, eventually, *The Basket* was hung. In describing this work, Federico Borromeo expressed his great admiration for Caravaggio and tells of how he would have liked to have had another basket of fruit painted to act as a pendant (perhaps with the two San Clemente baskets in mind) only that he had not succeded in finding a painter able to equal "huius pulchritudinem, incomparabilemque excellentiam", that is to say the beauty and incomparable excellency of this painting. Borromeo wrote about Caravaggio's basket: "flores micant" ("flowers abound"). The apparent lapsus (the basket contained fruit not flowers) can be explained by the common habit of calling the mystic bunches of grapes *flores vineae*, inspired by the *Song of Songs*. Borromeo himself, in annotating the same lines of the *Song* transcribed in Caravaggio's painting in the Doria Gallery ("videamus si flores fructus parturiunt"), observes that, even if it is not true that fruit grows out of flowers, there is in this idea a *poetic* truth, and that the expression "flowers of the vine" has a deeper meaning since the Groom (that is Christ) is both flower and fruit together. What better than this spontaneous flow of Borromeo's to demonstrate the sacred significance of the nonetheless naturalistic fruit which makes up Caravaggio's baskets? But this was never really understood. On the contrary, it was always believed that Borromeo's "mistake" was in fact a symptom of the Cardinal's considerable indifference for Caravaggio's paintings. According to this 'reading', Borromeo never actually commissioned or bought any of Caravaggio's works; he received them as gifts from Cardinal Del Monte. Evidence to support this was sought in a letter which, as a matter of fact, was later proved to have nothing to do with the question.

Supper in Emmaus *(c. 1600), detail. London, National Gallery.*

**The resurrected Christ is a youth with an androgynous face, half male, half female as in the Paleo-Christian images of the Good Shepherd, and not the mature man one would expect of one of his age. His youth is a sign of the eternal life which Christ offers to his followers.**

Basket of Fruit
*(c. 1600). Milan,
Pinacoteca Ambrosiana.*
**This work belonged
as early as 1607 to
Cardinal Federico
Borromeo, for whom
it was almost
definitely painted.
He adored still lives,
a genre which was
just developing at the
time; the Flemish Jan
Brueghel painted
many *still lives* of
vases of flowers for
the Cardinal.
Here, the image we
have already seen in
the *Youth* in the
Borghese Gallery, in
*Bacchus* and in *Supper
in Emmaus*, returns
isolated. Together
with the sense of
vigorous growth in
the "three
dimensionality" of
the description, we
have the elegance of
the placing of the
fruit, the sense of
measure which
contains the vigour
and which retains
something of the
Renaissance balance
and plastic luminosity
of an artist such as
Antonello da
Messina. The light
which seems to come,
unnaturally, from
more than one source
is like a lifegiving
breath which moves
the twigs and leaves
and turns colour into
perfume.**

# The Roman altarpieces

Deposition
*(1602-1604). Rome, Pinacoteca Vaticana.*
**Caravaggio undertook this work, one of his first altarpieces, for the church of Santa Maria in Vallicella in 1602. The wrinkles which mark the Virgin's face show the realism with which the artist represents his humble protagonists. In this work produced for public devotion, one can clearly see the difference as compared to the suave paintings undertaken for private commissions. The contrast between light and shade has become dramatic in this interpretation of a subject which evokes the passion of Christ.**

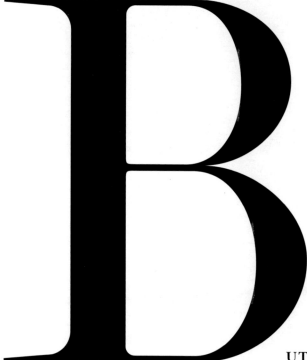

UT WHY WAS everyone so loath to admit that Borromeo might have been interested in Caravaggio? The fact is that Cardinal Federico was one of the most important and strictest exponents of the Catholic Counter-Reformation, the ideals of which were in diammetric opposition to Caravaggio's, or so people wanted to believe.

This is a particularly serious error because Caravaggio *did* in some way interpret (however individualistically) an innovative wing of the Counter-Reformation, the "pauperistic" wing headed by Borromeo and the Oratorians. This school of thought wished for a return of the Church to the purity, and therefore to the sobriety and poverty, of its beginnings. This was in direct contrast to the generalised Renaissance magnificence. The Oratorian Baroni went so far as to proclaim the falsity of Constantine's gift; Constantine who was the very pillar of the temporal power of the Church. Borromeo's pauperism is one of the characteristics Manzoni built on in his famous reconstruction of the Cardinal in the *Promessi Sposi*: in the novel he would always speak to "the roughest and most derelict of men" and would caress "sweaty and nauseating children". "He wanted his table to be not frugal, but positively impoverished. His clothing was not simple but positively pauper-like». This is by no means all invention, as one can see in contemporary reports.

One should even ask oneself if Bellori's picturesque and denigratory descriptions of Caravaggio's way of dressing, eating and living in general might not be a result of similar circumstances? "Let us not forget to mention his deportment and way of dressing. He would drape himself with noble velvets and fine cloths, but once he had put something on, he would never take it off, until it actually fell to tatters. He hardly ever washed and he ate for years and years on a portrait canvas, using it as a tablecloth from dawn to dusk".

Whatever, Caravaggio, during his early youth in Milan, must have lived in the shadow of that popular and very strict religion introduced by San Carlo which was particularly suited to the Lombard spirit, so full of social interest for the world of the poor and rejected.

What is more, Cardinal Federico must have been one of the artist's old aquaintances. He was, in fact, a relation of Costanza Colonna, Marquess of Caravaggio, for whom Caravaggio's father

Saint Matthew and the Angel *(c. 1601). Formerly Museum of Berlin, destroyed in the last World War.*

Saint Matthew and the Angel *(1602). Rome, Church of San Luigi de' Francesi.*
**Caravaggio had been accused by ecclesiastical circles of having little "decorum" in his** *Tales of Saint Matthew* **in the church of San Luigi de' Francesi. As a result of this criticism, the painter was probably obliged to re-paint the altarpiece.
The first version was wonderful: it represented Saint Matthew in the semblance of a rough, illiterate peasant staring in amazement at his own writing, physically guided by the Angel's hand.
The second version of Saint Matthew writing the Gospel is the one still to be seen to this day above the altar of the Contarelli Chapel. The saint has become a learned man, inspired, but not materially led, by the Angel.**

**On the following page:** Vocation of Saint Matthew *(1599-1600). Rome, Church of San Luigi de' Francesi.*
**Matthew, is redeemed by Christ by being called into the Apostolate. By repenting, even a sinner can be dipped in the light of Salvation. The light (symbol of Grace) emanated by Christ with Peter (symbol of the Church) by his side, shines on the "doomed mass" of men; but it is up to the individual to decide between Grace and Perdition. This was the Catholic theory which opposed that of French Protestants. The Huguenots believed that Salvation had nothing to do with Man's free will but with Predestination. In order to understand the importance of this debate, one must consider that the church of San Luigi de' Francesi represented the French Nation and that the King of France, the Huguenot Henry IV, had just been converted to Catholicism.**

worked, and whose family continued to protect Caravaggio through all his various misadventures. Borromeo was also a good friend of his colleague Del Monte, to whom he was tied by similar taste in pictures (as we can see if we compare their two private collections) and by their shared interest in science. When Federico Borromeo left Rome in 1595, he left the directorship of the Academy of San Luca to Del Monte. It is highly probable, furthermore, that Caravaggio first met Del Monte through Borromeo, or through Colonna. Caravaggio was also mentioned with regard to some contact which it is now impossible to clarify in a letter of 1607 received by Borromeo while the artist was in Malta. Finally, it is almost certain that Merisi's introduction into the Roman Society of the Oratorians (or Filippini) took place thanks to an indication of Cardinal Federico who was practically a member of the Oratorians (or at least he was very much at home there). In 1597 he financed the construction of the main altar in the Church of the Filippini, Santa Maria in Vallicella. In 1602, Caravaggio undertook one of his first altarpieces there: the *Deposition* (now in the Pinacoteca Vaticana), completed in 1604. The difference between the delicate paintings for private commissions or anyway not specifically for altars, and a work such as this is more than surprising. Any trace of pleasurableness has been wiped away.

The contrast between light and shade is deeply dramatic. The subject interpreted evokes that of the Passion of Christ.

The plastic potency of the group is heightened by this contrast and by the tight monolithic grouping of the protagonists placed one by one like steps, from Maria of Cheofas's upwards-reaching gesture which mirrors the cross, to the Virgin's half-raised hand, to Christ whose hand hangs down like a plumb-line touching the sepulchral stone. Under the stone, which alludes to Christ himself, the "corner-stone" of the Church (or according to some theologians, its foundation stone), sprouts a green plant, symbol of the resurrection, which is in antithesis to another dried-up plant in the opposite corner: again, we see the same sharp contrast as between light and shade.

The counterpoint to the idealised abstraction of the light is the realism with which the Virgin's wrinkles have been painted, presenting a picture of pained humanity; also the figure of Saint Joseph of Arimathea, with his peasant's face, his eyes sunk into the shadow, his rough, powerful legs full of veins. Chrsist's message is to the poor and the humble on whom the light of Salvation shines.

All this, however, outside Oratorian circles, must have seemed exceedingly lacking in "decorum".

Caravaggio had already been accused of lack of decorum when he painted, between 1599 and 1602, the *Tales of Saint Matthew* in the Contarelli Chapel in San Luigi de' Francesi.

It was probably because of this criticism that Caravaggio was forced to re-paint the altarpiece with *Saint Matthew and the Angel.* The first version was wonderful. It represented the saint writing the Gospel in the person of a rough illiterate peasant: he sits and watches his own writing guided by the hand of the angel, in amazement. Sadly, the painting, housed in Berlin, was destroyed in the Second World War.

The second version is that which can still be seen in the church: the saint has been transformed into an erudite man, inspired – but not materially guided – by the angel; the angel is no longer by his side, but up above him. The saint turns towards him, as if surprised by the divine Voice, but not excessively amazed; his face is scorched and signed, but it is certainly not rough. The two lateral canvases, on which Caravaggio painted the *Vocation* of the Saint and his *Martyrdom,* are also stupendously inventive.

The *Vocation of Saint Matthew* is equivalent to a conversion. Matthew, as the Gospels declare, was a "publican and a sinner" but he was redeemed by Christ and called to be an Apostle. Through repentance even a reprobate can be bathed in Christ's light which is the light of Salvation. Following the verse-comment made by Marzio Milesi, a friend of the painter's, the apparition of Christ "clears and brightens" Matthew's mind which is "cluttered and blind, tied up in tight knots".

Matthew was a tax collector, and the money on view on the table is a symbol of terrestrial greed. Those, like Matthew and the two well-dressed young men, who look up towards Christ (that is, they notice his light entering the room) will be saved. The others, such as the old bespectacled man and the third young man who goes on avidly counting money, don't answer his call, and are doomed to perdition. "Si qui non illuminantur", wrote the Jesuit Juan Maldonado (who died in 1583) concerning Grace, "quia recipere oblatum lumen nolunt, ideo non illuminari" ("if some are not illuminated, it is because they do not want to receive the light which has been offered; that is, they do not want to be illuminated"). Christ, in the *Gospel According to Saint John*, is "the true light which illuminates every man", but "the shadows do not receive light". Light (symbol of Grace), emanated by Christ together with Peter (symbol of the Church), shines on all men ("Massa peccati, iniquitatis, perditionis", that is, a "doomed mass" according to Saint Augustine), and offers them the possibility of Salvation. But it is up to each individual to choose whether to obey Christ or not; to choose between Grace and Perdition. This was the Catholic Theory which was in diammetric opposition to that of the French Protestants, or Huguenots, who strongly believed that Salvation was predestined and had nothing to do with man's free will.

In order fully to understand the importance of this debate one must take into consideration the fact that the church of San Luigi represented the French nation and that the King of France, Henry IV, had just been converted (with far-reaching political consequences) from the Huguenot to the Catholic faith. Henry IV was solemnly absolved by the Pope with a papal bull dated 1595 which contains a reference to the theme of light and shade taken up by Caravaggio. Just like Matthew, Henry IV had emerged from the shadow of sin to enter the light of Salvation. "You died for your sins", states the papal bull, "but the Lord brought you to life in Christ. We can see the overabundance of divine Grace in your conversion and reflect on the fact that – from the darkest obscurity of your errors and your heresy, thrown into an abyss of evil – thanks to a powerful act of the Lord's right hand, you have come to the light of Truth".

The powerful act of the Lord's right hand is recalled by Caravaggio (quoting from Michelangelo) in Christ's imperious gesture, when he points with his right hand at Matthew. Matthew, still dubious, points at himself as if to say : "Who? Me?". The extraordinary orchestration of light and shadow manages to communicate both the abstraction and idealism of the symbol and the true to life reality of the situation.

In the *Martyrdom*, the light forms a wedge which splits open the shadow, violently highlighting in the centre the ruffian who has thrown Matthew down at the bottom of the altar and slit him open. Blood pours out from his ribs like Christ, whose Passion is thus re-enacted. The symbolic sacrifice of the Mass which Matthew was celebrating is concluded and explicated by the cruel event, which causes an eruption of light. An angel from on high breaks through the shadow, offering the palm-leaf of martyrdom to Matthew's outstretched hand. The light on the right-hand side of the painting sharply sculpts the young boy's scream of horror as he seeks refuge, and on the other side the incredu-

Martyrdom of Saint Matthew *(1599-1600), whole painting and details. Rome, Church of San Luigi de' Francesi.*

**In contrast to the orderly composition of the *Vocation*, we have the *Martyrdom of Saint Matthew* which reveals an outburst of almost dionysiac agitation caused both by fears and by revelation. Even the murderer is invested by divine Grace which showers down tumultuosly on him, reflecting the dazzling intensity of mercy. Out of the undulating, awe-stricken crowd, on the left-hand side of the painting, peers the pained face of the painter, who ideally participates in the sacrifice of the Saint and in the salvation which will doubtless ensue.**

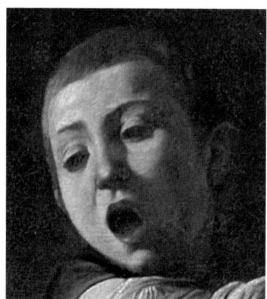

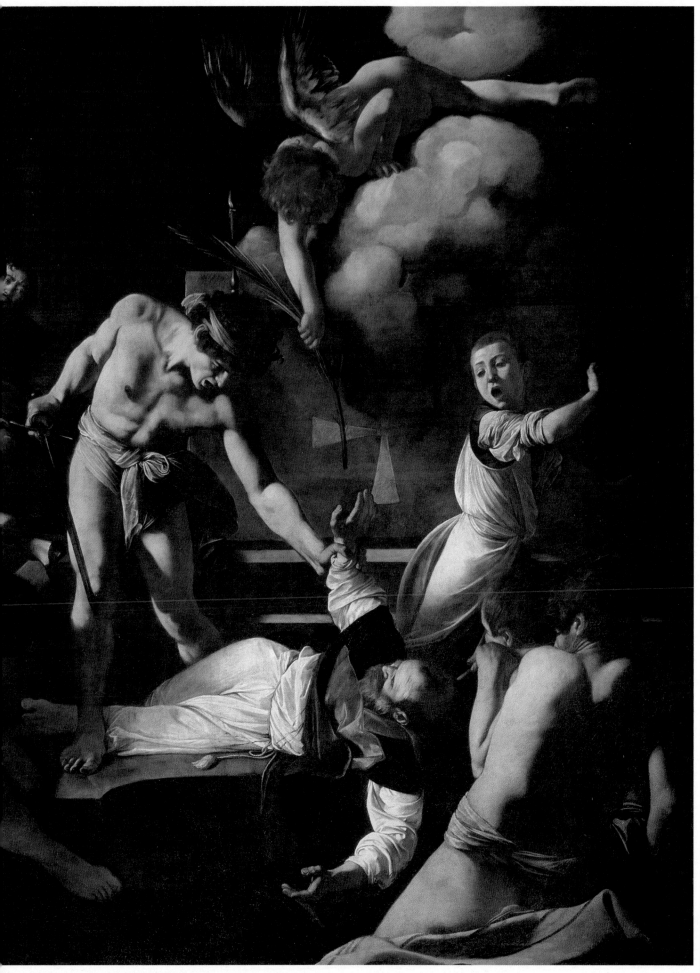

lous crowd undulates. Out of the background of the painting stares the pained face of the painter who presides over his work as the figure of *pietas*.

In contrast to the well-constructed composition of *Saint Matthew's Vocation*, and to the solemn tranquillity of the diffused ray of light which shines on the room, in the *Martyrdom* there is a visible agitation. This almost dionysiac agitation, however, is not only caused by fear: it is also a sign of revelation.

The murderer himself, on whose face one can also detect wonder, seems as though possessed by amazement at the sacred mystery. The light which radiates from the saint strikes him with its dazzling intensity of mercy. Divine Grace, as in *The Vocation*, also descends – tumultuous and overwhelming – on sinners, and if they recognize her they will be saved. Again Manzoni's words come to mind in "Cardinal Federico's (Borromeo's) meeting with the Innominato": God is kind to sinners, He loves them and is ready to forgive them as soon as they ask it of Him; they will receive "a consolation which is full, immense, as soon as they recognise Him".

X-rays demonstrate that Caravaggio re-painted the scene twice. The version which survives to this day is the third: entirely different to the others, much more dramatic and agitated. This proves that the artist did not made preparatory drawings, but that he drew as he painted, with an incredible plastic clarity which was not so much the fruit of lengthy preparations as the result of a spontaneous overflow, revealing his instantaneous and infallible capacity for evocation. In the same period as his activity in San Luigi de' Francesi the painter worked on the decoration, consisting in two paintings of the Cerasi Chapel in Santa Maria del Popolo between 1600 and 1601. The subjects are *The Conversion of Saint Paul* and *The Crucifixion of Saint Peter*.

An early version of *The Conversion of Saint Paul* (in the Odescalchi collection), later substituted by the present-day version, showed a

Conversion of Saint Paul
*(1600-1601), detail. Rome, Odescalchi Balbi Collection.*

During the same period as the work in San Luigi de' Francesi, Caravaggio undertook the lateral paintings in the Cerasi chapel, Santa Maria del Popolo. The first version of the *Conversion of Saint Paul* shows the figure of Eternity, hurling himself against the future apostle, fallen off his horse. Maybe the audacious representation of such an impetuous God was what was not liked in the painting.

Conversion of Saint
Paul
*(1600-1601). Rome,
Odescalchi Balbi
Collection.*

figure erupting out of Eternity, attacking the future Apostle who had fallen off his horse with the well-known phrase "Saul, Saul, why dost thou persecute me?". In the later version, this figure disappears and all the clamour of the previous painting calms down to an extraordinary stillness. The light, emanating from an invisible source, showers from on high and streams down the stupendous body of the horse, which acts almost as a reflector, bathing Paul's upturned body and flooding his face.

The symbolic meaning is more than obvious: it is the light of Grace shining on a sinner. The church of Santa Maria del Popolo belonged to the Augustinian Order, and for Saint Augustine – the greatest theoretician of Grace – knowledge is pure "vision in God", perpetual illumination: knowledge itself, in Augustinian philosophy is the light of Grace, a gift which shines down from on high. The raised arms of the converted persecutor hint at the completion of a circle or of an eclipse, together with the body of the animal who lowers its head to contemplate him, pulling down the groom's hand.

Lights flows inside the magic circle, transcending in a high point of revelation the nonetheless careful naturalistic rendering of the group. In the *Crucifixion of Saint Peter*, the light follows the serpentine line along which the crucifix is solemnly erected. Symbolically, this represents the erection of the Church which Christ founded in Peter and which his own martyrdom helps construct.

The dark, gruff figures of the crucifiers with their raven-black hair form a contrast with the serene expression of the saint, haloed by his grey hair. Saint Peter looks with proud strength at his punish-

Conversion of Saint Paul
*(1601). Rome, Church of Santa Maria del Popolo.*
**This later version of the painting eliminates all traces of desecration: it leaves room for the light, emanated from an invisible source, which is an obvious symbol of Grace descending on sinners.**

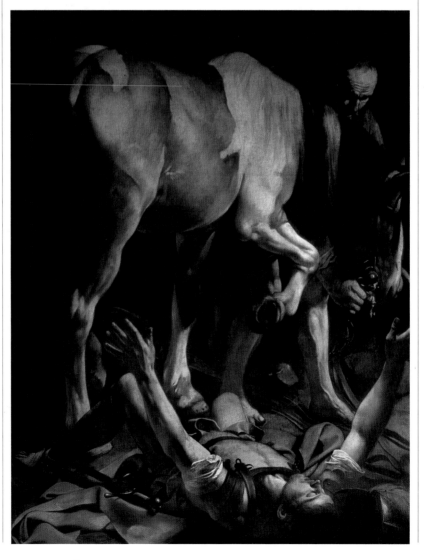

In the painting opposite, the theory of illuminating Grace formulated in Saint Augustine's writings returns once again. The light follows the serpentine line along which the cross is solemnly raised, whilst all around the "night" of sin thickens. The light of salvation irradiated by Peter illuminates even his murderers.

Crucifixion of Saint
Peter *(1601). Rome,
Church of Santa Maria
del Popolo.*

Madonna of Loreto
or Madonna
of the Pilgrims
*(1604). Rome, Church
of Sant'Agostino.*
**In this painting,
Caravaggio abandons
the traditional image
of the Virgin in flight
with her house
transported by the
angels. Mary is
portrayed on the
threshold of her
humble dwelling with
its crumbling
plasterwork, lovingly
showing Jesus to the
devoted pilgrims. In
the foreground we
can see the peasant's
dirty feet which
outraged those who
considered
Caravaggio's work
lacking in
"decorum".**

ment and stoically faces his suffering. The light which radiates from Peter (symbol of the Church and "imitator of Christ" in his martyrdom) is again the light of salvation. Even the murderers die illuminated, whilst all around the "night", or shadow of unredeemed sin, thickens.

The *Madonna of Loreto*, or *Madonna of the Pilgrims* in the Roman church of Sant'Agostino, goes back to 1604. The Madonna of Loreto was usually painted in flight together with the house where Jesus was born, transported "miraculously" by the angels from Palestine. Caravaggio, on the other hand, painted her on the threshold of the sacred habitation with its crumbling plaster to demonstrate her poverty. The only very vague hint of her flying is in her delicate way of standing tip-toe as if she were suspended.

The Virgin, peering out of the shadow on the threshold of light, is statuesque and yet palpitating and brimful of loving sentiments towards the pilgrims who have come to adore her. Her beauty contrasts with the plebeian features of the two devotees who symbolically represent the whole of humanity – a man and a woman, like Adam and Eve. In the foreground one can see the pilgrim's feet, dirty and worn after the long journey. Needless to say, critics who considered Caravaggio's painting lacking in "decorum" jumped on these details as evidence of their opinion. But we know that Caravaggio's passionate intention was to celebrate the poor and humble. Bare feet, as Federico Borromeo wrote in his

Madonna of the Horse-Grooms or Madonna of the Serpent *(1606). Rome, Borghese Gallery.*
**The only commission Caravaggio ever obtained from the Roman clergy (and not from religious orders) was this piece for the altar of the Confraternity of Horse-Grooms in Saint Peter's. The subject is the suppression of the diabolical serpent of Original Sin. No sooner was the work hung than it was withdrawn, almost certainly under orders of the new Pope Paul V, who was hostile towards the "pauperist" circles in which Caravaggio moved.**

*De Pictura Sacra,* are a symbol of obedience and faithfulness. Obedience and faithfulness in poverty and simplicity.

Up to this point, Caravaggio had worked for the Augustinians (who ran the churches of Santa Maria del Popolo and Sant'Agostino), for the Oratorians or for the priests of San Luigi (the church of the French). The clergy, that is the official Church of Rome, had always kept him at a distance.

The first and last commission of this other kind, though it ended up in the private collection of Scipione Borghese, was the *Madonna and the Serpent,* or the *Madonna of the Horse-Grooms.*

The subject of the painting, based on a passage from the Old Testament, is the suppression of the serpent of original sin. This was a subject of heated debate at the time between Roman Catholics and German Protestants.

The former declared that it was the Virgin who quelled the serpent (i.e. the Church quelling sin); the latter claimed that it was Jesus who did it (i.e. in order to obtain redemption from sin, one can apply directly to divine benevolence, without recourse to the mediation of the Roman Church).

Pope Pius IV in 1569 had in fact emitted a Papal bull in which it was established that the serpent had been suppressed by the Virgin together with her Son, thus identifying Protestant heresy in the figure of the serpent.

Caravaggio faithfully visualised this philosophy: the Madonna places her foot on the serpent's head while Jesus presses down on her foot to help her squash it. Next to her is Saint Anne, the Virgin's mother, who watches the scene impersonating in her ageing features mortal humanity which benefits from the event. No sooner was the painting hung over the altar than it was taken away, most likely by Pope Paul V (elected in 1605) who, not by chance, was particularly hostile towards the pauperists. Caravaggio, not surprisingly, was never again asked to produce a new version.

This was for him a condemnation with no Court of Appeal and – significantly – the same thing happened with his *Death of the Virgin,* painted for the church of Santa Maria della Scala, which belonged to the Order of the Discalced Carmelites. The work was rejected, and ended up in the Duke of Mantua's private collection in 1607. It later passed to the Louvre Museum.

The painting is one of Caravaggio's masterpieces. The Virgin, surrounded by the weeping Apostles, under a red drape which gives a theatrical air to the gloomy and humble room invaded by shadow, lies supine on a bare bier. Her face is beautiful, but extinguished by the breath of death; her left hand falls in abandon towards the observer; her right-hand rests on her abdomen which looks swollen.

Probably, under all this there lies a symbolism: the Virgin (portrayed as a young woman whereas in fact she was much older when she died) is a symbolic figure for the Church, as is often true in the tradition and almost invariably so (apart from the *Deposition* in the Pinacoteca Vaticana) in Caravaggio's paintings. The swollen abdomen alludes to Mary's being "full of Grace", always pregnant with Divine Grace, that is with the body of Christ. Surrounding her are the Apostles, overwhelmed by grief but illuminated by her light. They are positioned in such a way as to form – together with the Virgin's arm – a cross placed transversally, and they are the humble witnesses to the event taking place in the painting, which is incredibly simple and undecorated.

It is this very rejection of opulence which most characterises the religious circles close to Caravaggio: we have already recalled that Federico Borromeo was a friend to the poor. We know that he put up beggars in his house, and that he demonstrated how parsimoniously he lived by furnishing his house with very few rustic items. From his Cardinal's suite, through a secret door, one

Death of the Virgin (1606), *detail. Paris, Louvre Museum.*

reached a bare room with no more than a rough wooden table and a crucifix, a straw-bottomed chair and a sack on two stands on which to sleep.

It reminds one of the deeply suggestive bare surroundings in *Death of The Virgin*. But if this was the sense behind the representation, it was certainly not understood, or nobody wanted to understand it. The Virgin's pregnancy was considered a scandalous detail, and rumour had it that Caravaggio had even used as a model for the painting a prostitute who had drowned in the River Tiber.

**This is one of Caravaggio's masterpieces but it was not appreciated by the Discalced Carmelites of Santa Maria della Scala, for whom it was painted.**

**The "swollen" appearance of the Virgin was considered outrageous. Rumour had it that the painter had used a prostitute drowned in the River Tiber as his model.**

# The years
# on the run

Madonna
of the Rosary
*(1606). Vienna,
Kunsthistorisches
Museum.*
**After his flight from
Rome, Caravaggio
went to Naples where
he painted this
*Madonna of the Rosary*
with Saints Dominic
and Peter the Martyr.
It was commissioned
by Luigi Carafa
Colonna for the
family chapel in San
Domenico Maggiore.
The subject was
supposed to celebrate
the Victory of
Lepanto against the
Turks (1571) and
therefore the father
and grandfather – the
famous Marcantonio
Colonna – of the
commissioner who
fought in the battle.**

**T**HIS EPISODE, ON the other hand, crossed paths with Caravaggio's homicide, committed on the 28th of May 1606, since *Death of the Virgin* – almost certainly the last painting of the Roman period – was probably completed just before that terrible event which might well have contributed to its rejection, or at least have presented an obstacle for the commission of a further version.

In hiding in the estates of the Colonna at Paliano (run by Cardinal Ascanio Colonna, brother of the Marquess of Caravaggio, and by Filippo Colonna, son of Anna Borromeo, Cardinal Federico's cousin), according to contemporary biographers, Caravaggio painted a *Mary Magdalen* filled with a new dramatic pathos which has been identified today in a private collection in Rome.

In Naples, as early as the first days of October, he painted (most probably commissioned by Luigi Carafa-Colonna, the Marquess of Caravaggio's nephew, for the family chapel in San Domenico Maggiore) the *Madonna of the Rosary* with Saints Dominic and Peter the Martyr.

The Rosary holiday had been instituted to celebrate the great victory of Lepanto against the Turks, on the 7th of October, 1571. This painting, therefore, dates to the thirty-fifth anniversary of the legendary event in which Marcantonio Colonna, the Marquess of Caravaggio's father and Luigi Carafa-Colonna's grandfather, fought together with the latter's father, Antonio Carafa. If one compares this painting with the altarpieces of the Roman period, the composition of the group of devotees who pray to Saint Dominic is incredibly cram-packed, whilst Saint Peter the Martyr (with a head-wound from a sword, exactly like the painter who must still have had visible signs of his) points at the solemn but maternal Virgin holding the Holy Child. In the heavy harmony in tone created by the light, a resonant note is produced by the huge red drape, tied emphatically round the massive column which almost definitely alludes to the clan of Victors at Lepanto. Despite the crowding of the figures, the structure is nevertheless tight and luminously plastic.

There is an obvious change, however, in the representation of the *Seven Works of Mercy,* for which Caravaggio was paid on the 9th of January, 1607, by the Neapolitan Confraternity of Pio Monte to whom the work was destined. The painting is divided into different clusters of activity, and the link is provided by the background

*Seven Works
of Mercy
(1606-1607). Naples,
Church of Pio Monte
della Misericordia.*
**The scene seems to
take place in the
hustle and bustle of a
crowded popular
street in Naples. And
yet all this naturalism
serves to veil the
choice of subjects
which illustrate the
evangelical works of
mercy in a tapestry of
marvellous mastery.
One can note the
spirit of the return to
the Gospel by the
emblematic everyday
images taken from
the Bible and the
Classics.**

where the varying intensities of light (from the shadow of total vacuum, to the walls of the building either in *penombra* or well-lit) articulate at intervals the space.

In the lower part of the painting the figures seem to want to slip back into the shadow, whilst from above the miraculous whirlpool of wings, drapery and limbs through which the faces of Jesus and Mary transpire, together with the sculptured projection of the angels, radiantly errupts out of the darkness.

It has been said, quite rightly, that the scene seems to present the hustle and bustle of a popular street in Naples. But only much later was it understood that all this naturalism served to veil a careful choice of subjects suitable for illustrating the theme of the painting – that is the Seven Works of Mercy – mixed together in a tapestry of marvellous mastery.

On the right we have: "burying the dead" (transporting a corpse, of which we see only the feet); "visiting prisoners" and "feeding the needy" (works which are both to be found in the classical episode of Cimon dying in prison lovingly breast-fed by his daughter Pero).

On the left: "clothing the poor" (Saint Martin who gives half of his cloak to a beggar); "taking care of the infirm" (Saint Martin also cured a young cripple, visible behind the pauper); "giving the thirsty to drink" (Samson drinks the water which the Lord miraculously called forth from an ass's jaw in the middle of the desert); and finally "offering lodgings to pilgrims" (alluding to the man indicating a hostel to a traveller, portrayed as Saint James of Compostela).

For years, none of these scenes were understood. Bellori describes the realistic but refined figure of Samson as that of "one who, lifting his glass up to his lips, drinks with his mouth open rudely dribbling wine". Re-reading Bernard Berenson's comment, written in 1951 (incidentally, he too mistook the ass's jaw for a cup) one realises the superficial approach even of modern criticism: "What can one say of a composition such as the *Seven Works of Mercy* in which one sees only the corpse's feet carried off for burial, a young hysterical woman proferring her breast to an old man, a few Giorgionesque figures engaged in indecipherable activities and a man (presumably a doctor) who looks at the contents of a glass against the light?"

People either found in it a confirmation of Caravaggio's eccentricity, or else they tried to demonstrate how Caravaggio eluded the subjects imposed on him by the commission and portrayed instead scenes which he happened to come a cross wandering through the streets of Naples, thus scorning the original religious import of the work.

To the contrary, it is precisely in the *Seven Works* that one can detect an agreement with the *Catechism* signed by Cardinal Roberto Bellarmino in 1597 and a newly aroused interest in the Gospel, suggested by the use of "lowly" figures in the painting, emblematic images taken from the repertory of the Bible and the Classics.

The *Flagellation*, also painted in Naples for the church of San Domenico Maggiore, is powerfully tragic. The massive bodies no longer have that plastic three-dimensionality of the Roman period; the layers of light in which they are enveloped sink heavily into the shadow.

But Naples cannot have been a safe enough refuge for the fugitive artist; possibly the Colonna family themselves suggested that he should go to Malta, where he landed probably on the 12th of July, 1607, on a galley-ship commanded by the General of the Fleet of the Order of Saint John, Fabrizio Colonna: not by chance, the Marquess of Caravaggio's son.

A year after his arrival in La Valletta, on the 14th of July, 1608, the painter was admitted into the Order as a knight, in recognition of

the merit he had earned for his activity on the island.

Von Sandrart mentions his "courageousness against the Turks", and it is anything but impossible that Caravaggio did take part – on Fabrizio Colonna's ship – in some military action; there were after all an infinite number of attacks which that "foreign legion" at the frontiers of Christianity had to face. The very document of admission into the knighthood, moreover, speaks of his "religious zeal".

However, his most important merit was as a painter and Caravaggio didn't miss the opportunity of painting a portrait of the Gran Maestro of the Order, Alof de Wignacourt. The painting, now in the Louvre, presents a certain contrast between the communicative naturalism of the face and the conventional pose of the body, enclosed in antique-style armour, easily datable to the 1570's. Wignacourt himself, it must be remembered, took part in the Battle of Lepanto (1571) and the armour obviously refers to this glorious period and is presented in a deliberately emblematic and almost heraldic way.

The Gran Maestro's face has also been recognised in the ascetic *Saint Jerome* which, until the recent shameful theft, was kept in the Cathedral Museum in Malta. While on the one hand the portrait in the Louvre refers to Wignacourt's military exploits, on the other this portrait might allude to the contemplative life which should always complement the "active" one.

The order of Malta, in fact, was also a religious order, inspired by the rule of Saint Augustine. Caravaggio, as we mentioned previously, signed his supreme Maltese masterpiece "f(rà) Michel Angelo": *The Beheading of Saint John,* painted for the *Compagnia della Misericordia* which ran the Oratory where the huge canvas (360 cms long) was hung and where it can be seen to this day. That is, the Oratory of the convent church of the Knights of Saint John in La Valletta (today the Cathedral).

Looking at this work one remains speechless: the effect is so powerful that it both moves and transcends one. One cannot look at the signature without shivering, because that signature is drawn from the red pool of blood that flows from the trunk of the beheaded Saint. The dramatic effect immediately reminds one of the painter's existence and the weight of the capital sentence which constantly persecuted him. This was a secret which very soon was to be discovered, causing his arrest, his consequent evasion and then his escape across Sicily.

The light which bounces off the figures, evokes the last palpitations of life left in the martyr's body, lying face downwards with his hands tied behind his back. It is the culminating moment of the action. The executioner, who has already inflicted the fatal sword-wound, is about to draw the short dagger, called a "misericord", to finish off the beheading with a *coup de grâce*. The young woman, Salomé, impatiently holds forth the tray on which the head is to be placed as the prison-guard's gesture commands, whilst the old woman is moved by pity and grief. The abandoned rope hanging from the ring on the wall, on the right-hand side of the painting, leaves to our imagination what might have taken place minutes before when the Saint was untied and pulled into the foreground.

The punishment takes place in the courtyard of the prison (Federico Borromeo, in his *De Pictura Sacra* recommended painters always to "portray the dark, dismal prison" when representing Saint John's martyrdom) and two other convicts spy on the scene through the grates of their cell.

The relationship between space and the figures has been modified compared to earlier paintings; the emptiness has been amplified and it is immersed in a mute *penombra*, which dramatises and modulates the Titian-like tones. The figures no longer have that

plasticity of old, painted with large-scale luminous registers, but seem to vibrate in the strands of light which shudder over the bodies, eating into their form.

The "misericord", exhibited almost in the centre of the painting, was certainly intended to recall the name of the Confraternity which commissioned the work and which probably had amongst its many tasks (as in all the Confraternities of Misericord) that of helping the death-row prisoners. One could not say that it was by chance that Caravaggio worked in Malta for this Confraternity, since in Naples he had worked for the Pio Monte della Misericordia. In fact, the "Orators" and the "Confraternities", together with all the other mendicant orders (Augustinians, Carmelites, Franciscans, Capuccins, and Dominicans) were the most assiduous commissioners of his works. This once again demonstrates how his "pauperist" painting was highly congenial to a few precisely defined religious circles.

The last work which can be attributed to the Maltese period is the *Annunciation*, at Nancy, which again offers to the viewer an interior stripped of any decoration, just as Caravaggio had imagined the Virgin's habitation to be like at her death.

The Sicilian paintings carry the artistic novelties expressed in the *Beheading* to an even further extreme. The *Burial of Saint Lucy*, painted in Syracuse, is again set against the rarefied backdrop of a massive wall, cut on the far left side into an arch, and filled-in for more than half the painting so that its mysteriously silent monotonality – like an acquarium of shadows – bears down on the crowd of people, almost wiped out by the tragic quivers of light.

The Saint's neck has been pierced by the mortal wound; but at first (as one can easily see by the brush-strokes) her head must have appeared completely detached. Caravaggio's existential involvement in the events he represented became increasingly intense and acute in his final years.

The almost obsessive frequency with which he paints beheadings cannot but be connected with his personal drama and with his nightmare of being condemned to death.

In the *Resurrection of Lazarus*, painted in Messina for the church of the Padri Crociferi, the ferment of light is almost delirious. It sparks and then fizzles out like so many brief bonfires struggling against the shadow which, pushing its way out of the background, attracts the figures towards it.

The light, like a cracking electric shock on Lazarus' stiff body, brings a breath of life back to him and makes him open his arms in a dramatic gasp, suspending across the gloomy dusk the sign of the cross of Salvation.

The person who commissioned this work dedicated to Lazarus was called significantly Giovan Battista de' Lazzari. And it was in this period that another Messinese commissioner, the abovemen-

Burial of Saint Lucy
(1608), detail. Syracuse,
Church of Santa Lucia.

Resurrection of Lazarus
*(1609). Messina, Regional Museum.*
**Undertaken for the Church of the Padri Crociferi in Messina, the work was later requested by a certain Giovan Battista de' Lazzari, as a homage to his family name. In this work the ferment of light is almost delirious: it is like an electric shock in Lazarus's still stiff body, which in a dramatic gasp, opens his arms, shaping the cross of salvation.**

Adoration of the Shepherds
*(1609). Messina, Regional Museum.*
**This other Messinese work is calmer: the figures are positioned so as to form an elementary cross, though the shape is very well hidden by the naturalness of their pose. This sign not only indicates salvation, but it also alludes to the bare simplicity of the poor for whom the Gospel was written.**

tioned Niccolò di Giacomo, wrote of Caravaggio "This painter is out of his mind". Much of this anxiety, which might well have appeared madness, can be read in the stylistic agitation of this worrying masterpiece.

The *Adoration of the Shepherds* (again painted in Messina) is calmer in tone. The six figures of the shepherds, Saint Joseph, the Virgin Mary and the Child are so positioned as to create the shape of an elementary cross, positioned diagonally and in perspective, though this fact is well hidden by the naturalness of their pose. The cross is not only a sign of salvation, it is also a sign of the bare simplicity of the poor, to whom the Gospel – both in word and in deed – is addressed. A further theft which took place in 1969 deprived Sicily of a final masterpiece: the *Nativity* of the Oratory of the Company of San Lorenzo, Palermo. This work, however, might have been painted elsewhere and only later transferred to that city. We do not in fact know for certain whether Merisi passed through Palermo or not. It is nonetheless highly probable that it is from there that he set sail for Naples in the late summer or early autumn of 1609.

Whatever the case may be, in August the painter was still in Messina; in October he was already in the capital city of Campania where he was almost certainly arrested, after being attacked

and badly wounded by a group of armed ruffians at the gates of a hostel. In the months which followed, Caravaggio went on working. This is not so unlikely when one considers that the Spaniards in Naples treated the prisoner with great respect, maybe hoping to take possession of his highly sought after paintings. We know for a fact that the Viceroy Juan Alonso Pimentel y Herrera, setting off for Spain in June 1610, took with him two of Caravaggio's paintings; two others were expropriated by Don Juan de Tasks y Peralta, who came to Naples in 1611. The new Viceroy De Castro, after the painter's death at Port'Ercole on the 18th of July, confiscated a painting found amongst Caravaggio's belongings, probably the *Salomè with the Head of the Baptist*, today in Madrid. One of the two paintings shipped to Spain by Pimentel was the *Crucifixion of Saint Andrew* (presently in the Museum of Cleveland) which represents another story which existentially moved Caravaggio.

The Saint, condemned to die on the cross to which he has been tied, refuses to be saved and prays to the Lord to free him of the "heavy burden" of his existence. The old man, his face and body melted like wax, is portrayed as he dies against a gloomy sky, crossed by a ray of light.

*Salomè* (en equally crude version of which can be found in the National Gallery, London) proposes yet again the obsessive theme of the beheading of Saint John, in a composition laconically locked inside heavy black shadow.

In the *Punishment of Saint Ursula* in the Banca Commerciale of Naples (a work which has been dated May 1610, but found only recently), the artist paints his own face behind that of the martyr's, thus becoming part of the dying body, pierced by an arrow. The "syntax" of the painting is dramatically reduced to a bare minimum: a blinking, emotional luminosity, barely outlined, which marks the passage from Titian to Rembrandt, but which is characterised by a dramatic interiorisation which belongs to neither and which, in fact, has no comparison in any other moment of the history of art. A playwright of the brush-stroke, Michelangelo da Caravaggio, if anything, could be compared to his contemporary: Shakespeare.

Caravaggio's swan-song was painted in the same months, or just before *Saint Ursula: David with the Head of Goliath*, recorded in the Borghese Gallery, Rome, as early as 1613.

The density of shadow which almost hides David's right arm from the shoulder downward and reduces the plastic solidity of his body, excludes the possibility of this work's belonging to the Roman period, and places it, instead, together with his last works. Caravaggio, therefore, must have sent it to Cardinal Scipione Borghese, the Pope's nephew, in Rome, alongside or following his application for mercy. Even though it is not his last work, Goliath's decapitated head – a self-portrait – is certainly a tragic farewell. This would have been Caravaggio's destiny, if the application for mercy had not been granted. David, according to the exegesis of the Church Fathers, is the figure of Christ. This reading is given substance when one looks at the expression of Christian "pity" on the boy's face as he looks at the severed head of the "sinner", hit right on the forehead by David's stone which leaves its bloody stain. In identifying himself with this figure, Caravaggio was admitting his guilt, but maybe he also wanted to remind the Pope, as if he were asking for extenuating circumstances, that in that terrible fight in 1606 he too was wounded in the head. Mercy was granted, but destiny was soon to take its predestined course, possibly because of his worsening health already tested after the armed agression a few months previous. His *coup de grâce* was the parching sun on the Feniglia beach near Port'Ercole, on the 18th of July, 1610.

A playwright with his brush-stroke, Caravaggio could be compared to his contemporary Shakespeare. His swan-song, this *David with the Head of Goliath* is one of the last works produced in Naples. The painter sent it to Rome to Cardinal Scipione Borghese, the Pope's nephew, probably included together with or following his application for mercy. Mercy was granted, but his previsaged destiny was fulfilled on the Feniglia beach near Port'Ercole, where the parching sun inflicted on him his final *coup de grâce*.

David with the Head
of Goliath
*(1610). Rome, Borghese
Gallery.*

# CHRONOLOGICAL TABLE

| HISTORICAL EVENTS | | CARAVAGGIO'S LIFE |
|---|---|---|
| Victory of the Christian fleet over the Turks at Lepanto | **1571** | Michelangelo Merisi born in Milan of Fermo and Lucia Aratori, 29th September (St. Michael Archangel's day) |
| The massacre of the Huguenots in France on St. Bartholemew's night | **1572** | |
| | **1577** | The Merisi family, to flee the plague, moves from Milan to Caravaggio; father and paternal grandparents die |
| San Carlo Borromeo, Archbishop of Milan dies | **1584** | Caravaggio starts his apprenticeship in Milan with the painter Simone Peterzano |
| Sixtus V becomes Pope (until 1590) | **1585** | |
| Mary Stuart condemned to death | **1587** | |
| Destruction of the Invincible Armada: English victory over Spain | **1588** | Apprenticeship with Peterzano completed |
| | **1590** | Caravaggio's mother dies |
| Clement VIII becomes Pope (until 1605) | **1592-1593** | Caravaggio at 21 moves to Rome. |
| Henry IV of France abjures Calvinism for Catholicism | **1593** | Possibly enters Cavalier d'Arpino's studio. Sent to the Hospital of the Consolation for an illness |
| | **1595-1596** | Taken in by his protector, Cardinal Del Monte, Ambassador of the Grand Duke of Tuscany to Rome |
| | **1599** | Caravaggio obtains his first public commission: the *Tales of St Matthew* in the church of San Luigi de' Francesi |
| Solemn festivities for the Jubilee year. Giordano Bruno burnt at the stake in Rome. Henry IV of France marries Maria de' Medici | **1600** | Receives commission for the two paintings in the Contarelli chapel, Santa Maria del Popolo |
| James I starts the Stuart dynasty. Academy of the *Lincei* is founded | **1603** | Trial against Caravaggio and other friends of the painter's for having libelled the painter Giovanni Baglione |
| | **1604-1605** | Caravaggio arrested many times for slander and illegal bearing of arms |
| After the brief spell as Pope of Leo XI, Pope Paul V is elected | **1605** | Flees to Genoa for about a month after wounding the notary-public Pasqualone |
| Pope Paul V launches the interdiction against the Republic of Venice | **1606** | The *Madonna of the Horse-Grooms* is withdrawn from St. Peter's; his *Death of the Virgin* is refused. The painter kills his adversary after a game; flees to the Colonna estates (Zagarolo and Paliano), then to Naples |
| | **1607-1608** | Stays in Malta, paints the enormous *Beheading of St. John*. Nominated Knight of the Order of Malta. Found to be a murderer, flees to Syracuse |
| Johannes Kepler publishes *Astronomia Nova* | **1609** | Escape continues, from Messina to Palermo to Naples; in the latter he is attacked and wounded in the face |
| King Henry IV is assassinated, Maria de' Medici regent to the French Throne. Carlo Borromeo proclaimed saint | **1610** | Having obtained the Pope's mercy, Caravaggio dies on the 18th July near Port'Ercole, on his way back to Rome |

**ACKNOWLEDGEMENTS** Giunti Publishing Group archives: book cover and all the illustrations; except those at pages: 10, 15, 16, 19, 32-33, 38-39, 40-41, 49, 52, 56-57, 61, 63, provided by Scala agency, Florence.

*Translation from italian by Clarissa Botsford Ruth Taylor*

www.giunti.it

© 1998 Giunti Editore S.p.A. Florence - Milan

Managing director Claudio Pescio

Periodical publication Reg. Cancell. Trib. Firenze n. 3384 del 22.11.1985

Printed by Giunti Industrie Grafiche S.p.A. Prato - Italy

V.A.T. paid by the publisher in accordance with the Article 74 lett. c - DPR 633 del 26.10.72

**Subscription Pubblication Art e Dossier** (for back numbers of both the journal and the supplement) Tel. 199 195 525 Monday - Friday 9.00 am - 6.00 pm Fax 055 5062397 Post office account. 12940508 in name of Art e Dossier, Firenze e-mail periodici@giunti.it purchases on line www.giuntistore.it